Liberating Learning:
Widening Participation

Liberating Learning:
Widening Participation

Edited by
Patrick Derham
and
Michael Worton

The University of Buckingham Press

First published in Great Britain in 2010 by

The University of Buckingham Press
Yeomanry House
Hunter Street
Buckingham MK18 1EG

ISBN 978 0 9560716 8 2

CONTENTS

Notes on Contributors   *i*

Introduction   *v*
Patrick Derham and Michael Worton

Universities and Schools: Learning Together to Liberate Learning   1
Michael Worton

Liberating Learning: Liberal Education   9
AC Grayling

The Decline of History and the Futures of Western Civilisation   15
Niall Ferguson

Science, History, and Philosophy   25
Simon Blackburn

Promoting Engagement with Science Education   29
Michael Reiss

Learning And Control: Towards an Improved Model for Curriculum   35
Development
Simon Lebus

Education for 21st Century Business   43
Stuart Rose and John May

The Perspectives Model for the EPQ   49
Elizabeth Swinbank and John Taylor

EPQ   55
Sarah Fletcher

Raising Aspirations by Mentoring   61
Nigel Bowles

"Home Is Where One Starts From": **Into**University and the Role of the   69
Home Environment in Pupil Achievement
Rachel Carr and Hugh Rayment-Pickard

Social Exclusion and Underachievement: The Eastside Story   75
Ray Lewis

Unleashing Aspiration   81
Patrick Derham

NOTES ON CONTRIBUTORS

Simon Blackburn is currently the Professor of Philosophy at the University of Cambridge and Fellow of Trinity College, Cambridge. From 1984-1990 he edited the journal *Mind*. He was elected Fellow of the British Academy in 2001 and Honorary Foreign Member of the American Academy of Arts and Sciences in 2008. His most recent books include: *Truth: A Guide* (2005), *Plato's Republic* (2006), *How to Read Hume* (2008), and *The Big Questions of Philosophy* (2009).

Nigel Bowles has a DPhil from Oxford University; is the Honor Balfour Fellow in Politics, St Anne's College, Oxford; Director of Graduate Studies (Politics), Department of Politics and International Relations, Oxford University and Director of the Rothermere American Institute, Oxford University. His most recent book is *Nixon's Business: Authority and Power in Presidential Politics,* (2005) which was the winner of the Richard Neustadt Prize, 2006.

Rachel Carr is one of the co-founders of **Into**University. Rachel devised and ran the programme before becoming Chief Executive in 2007. Previously she worked as a lecturer in the university sector.

Patrick Derham is Head Master of Rugby School, a Syndicate member of Cambridge Assessment and Deputy Chairman of the Trustees of **Into**University.

Niall Ferguson is Laurence A. Tisch Professor of History at Harvard University and the author of numerous books, most recently *The Ascent of Money: A Financial History of the World* (2008).

Sarah Fletcher is now Head at Kingston Grammar School. She was Director of Studies at Rugby School from 1999 to 2009 and Deputy Head from 2003. Her main interest lies in encouraging independent learning and in promoting creativity in teaching and learning. She has delivered a number of talks and written articles on best practice in the delivery of the Extended Project. She sits on the Steering Committee for the Cambridge Pre-U, having been involved in the development of the project from its inception.

AC Grayling is Professor of Philosophy at Birkbeck, University of London, a Supernumerary Fellow of St Anne's College, Oxford, and a Fellow of the Royal Society of Literature. He is the author of over twenty books, and is a frequent broadcaster and contributor to broadsheet newspapers.

Simon Lebus is Group Chief Executive of Cambridge Assessment and Chairman of the OCR exam board. After studying history at Oxford he had a variety of roles in finance and business before joining Cambridge Assessment in 2002. He is a Bye Fellow of Emmanuel College and a Board member of the Cambridge University Faculty of Education.

Ray Lewis is the Founder and Director of Eastside Young Leaders' Academy. He is the co-author of *Latchkey to Leadership: Channelling the Talents of Inner City Kids*.

John May is the Chief Executive of Young Enterprise, the UK's leading business and enterprise education charity. A former headteacher, John has worked with children and young people in a variety of situations, ranging from schools in suburban England to refugee camps in Uganda. In 2008, John received The Queen's Award for Enterprise Promotion in recognition of his long-standing dedication to enterprise education.

Hugh Rayment-Pickard led **Into**University as Chair of Trustees before becoming Director of Communications. He has 25 years' experience in the not-for-profit sector, has taught in the higher education sector and is author of several academic titles.

Michael Reiss is Assistant Director and Professor of Science Education at the Institute of Education, University of London, Chief Executive of Science Learning Centre London, Vice-President of the British Science Association, Honorary Visiting Professor at the Universities of Birmingham and York, Director of the Salters-Nuffield Advanced Biology Project, a member of the Farm Animal Welfare Council and editor of the journal *Sex Education*.

Sir Stuart Rose has worked in retail for over 30 years. He was named Chief Executive of Marks & Spencer plc in May 2004 and became Chairman in 2008. He is Chairman of Business in the Community and a Non-executive Director of Land Securities plc. Stuart was knighted in 2008 for services to the retail industry and corporate social responsibility.

Elizabeth Swinbank is a physicist who has taught at both school and university level. She is currently a Fellow in Science Education at the University of York where, in addition to working on "Perspectives on Science" (PoS) and the development of Extended Project Qualification (EPQ) resources, she directs the Salters Horners Advanced Physics project and chairs the editorial board of Physics Review magazine.

John Taylor is Director of Critical Skills at Rugby School. Before taking up his post at Rugby he tutored in the Philosophy of Science at Oxford University. Since 1999 he has directed the "Perspectives on Science" (PoS) project. Dr Taylor is also a Chief Examiner for the Extended Project.

Michael Worton is Vice-Provost and Fielden Professor of French Language at University College London. He is also Higher Education Advisor to the British Council, and the author of many books and articles on modern literature, gender and higher education.

INTRODUCTION

Patrick Derham and Michael Worton

Only the educated are truly free
Epictetus, 2nd Century AD

Education is the pathway to freedom, democracy and development
Nelson Mandela

Throughout the history of our civilization, education has been seen by philosophers and national leaders and by educators to be essential for social cohesion and for economic development. Added to this is the fact that a good experience of education greatly enhances the quality of life of students not only during periods of formal education, but also throughout their lives. There is, however, inevitably a certain tension between the (proper) interest of governments in ensuring that education will prepare all young people to be good and effective citizens and the desire of educators to ensure that the learning experience of each individual student is as rich and personally developmental as possible. It is, of course, important to have comparable standards within a single country and as far as possible between countries. However, this does not apply, we would argue, when it comes to issues of curriculum, where standardisation leads all too swiftly to constraint and over-heavy regulation.

The liberal tradition in education places great emphasis on individual freedom and its emphasis goes well beyond promoting "freedom from...", rather positioning and promoting education as "freedom to..." It is this commitment to education's emancipatory potential that underpins all the essays in this book. We focus on three key areas: the curriculum; pedagogy; and the role of secondary education in widening participation in higher education. We invited authoritative thinkers and practitioners to address these issues from different perspectives in order to generate a debate around how we can translate our shared vision of education as authentically enabling and emancipatory into a transformational reality for all young people.

The world of schools and universities is changing rapidly, as globalisation expands all possibilities of communication and mobility. New and emerging technologies are changing the ways that teaching and learning occur and, especially as social networking technologies evolve, the public and the private blur and merge; learning and socialising become closer and intertwined; hierarchies mutate and dissolve as students learn better to interrogate and to research, and take the opportunity to be part of the process of the creation and management of knowledge rather than simply the recipients of it.

Exciting work is taking place across the UK, as is evidenced from the essays in this volume. Significantly, there is increasing awareness of the need to share ideas and exchange good practice not only between different parts of the secondary schools sector, but also between the school sector and the University and the FE sector – and between educators and policy-makers. This book presents a variety of different pioneering initiatives with a series of commentaries from different perspectives on where education is and where it is going. We hope the often challenging insights of our distinguished contributors will serve as sign-posts to an educational landscape of greater diversity and greater autonomy for learners and teachers alike. We hope also that they will serve as catalysts for further debate on how we can work and think together truly to liberate learning and to widen participation in a lifelong adventure of learning.

UNIVERSITIES AND SCHOOLS: LEARNING TOGETHER TO LIBERATE LEARNING

Michael Worton

In his speech to the 1996 Labour Party conference, Tony Blair, then leader of the Opposition, set out his Party's agenda for Government, with the ringing word: "Ask me my three main priorities for Government, and I tell you: Education, Education, Education". The triple repetition made clear both to his Party and to the nation that education was to be the top priority of his Government - and from the moment that he took office as Prime Minister until he resigned, Tony Blair was to insist repeatedly that education was his Government's main concern – for both social cohesion and economic development reasons. This was reflected in the significant investment that followed, over a period of more than a decade, in schools and in universities, in teaching and research.

For many of us, Blair's "Education, Education, Education" was more than a simple piece of political rhetoric: it signalled a commitment not only to prioritising and properly funding education but also to seeing education as a holistic whole. This was an important step forward, as it suggested that we could and would move from conceiving of education in linear (yet determinedly discrete) terms as consisting of primary, secondary and tertiary education to a vision and a strategy of joining up education (just as Government was to be joined up). Nevertheless, we need to ask whether the high priority and significant investment given to both school and university education have genuinely led to the transformations in learning that so many had hoped for, particularly in the context of the relationship between the two sectors.

For the past decade, universities have indeed been working evermore closely with schools, notably in terms of widening participation, seeking to raise aspirations of all pupils, whatever their abilities and aptitudes, although with a special focus on students from lower socio-economic classes and from non-traditional backgrounds where there is no family history of university attendance. These aspiration-raising activities take many forms: for instance, university academics give talks, master-classes, etc in schools, and university students serve as classroom assistants, mentors, role models or buddies (both in real time and through email mentoring). Furthermore, school groups are increasingly often invited into universities for lectures, science demonstrations, drawing classes, theatre productions and summer schools. Significantly, these widening participation activities are now often defined more accurately as outreach activities, since they are ways of universities engaging with their local communities, as well as contributing to raising the aspirations of school-children and encouraging them to think of science and the arts and humanities in different and excitingly challenging ways. There has been a tremendous expansion in university engagement with schools in recent years, and the relationships and projects that develop are strong and successful. Yet, although much outreach work takes the school curriculum as its starting point, often we find it easier to speak of "enriching" what schools are already teaching, rather than seeking to work with our colleagues in the secondary sector truly to transform learning.

The DCSF publication *Butterflies for Higher Education Partnerships* (2009)[1] offers an interesting overview of the innovative relationships which are being forged in London and presents case studies which are representative of exciting partnerships between schools and universities across the country. Crucially, several of the case studies in this 2009 publication suggest that some collaboration is now beginning to move beyond traditional, "enrichment-driven" outreach activity, towards a collaborative approach to curriculum development at secondary level which harnesses the expertise and resources of all parties.

Imperial College, for instance, is working with Villiers High School and Exscitec to develop online physics, biology and chemistry materials for 11-14 year olds. These resources are designed by academics and students from Imperial, and include video clips, quizzes, learning games and online reference tools. Additionally, the project combines small group tutorials with practical activities led by Imperial College undergraduates; these are designed to encourage the school students to develop their thinking skills, and to put their knowledge into context in practical tasks. The younger students also have the opportunity to complete assignments "online", which are then marked by the undergraduates and returned with feedback. In this partnership, it is the complementarity of the partners which brings the greatest added value, combining the academic specialist knowledge from the university with the school's pedagogical expertise. This harnesses the resources of the university in

---

[1] See the *Butterflies for Higher Education Partnerships* (DCSF, Crown copyright, 2009). The publication is also available at:
http://www.lepawards.org.uk/documents/3966_Butterflies_Book_5.pdf (last accessed 24th January 2010).

a way which gives coherence and shape to the pupils' learning, and makes it directly relevant to their experiences in the classroom.

Another example is that of a partnership between Alexandra Park School and the Physics and Astronomy Department at UCL, which developed from a standard "masterclass" model into a sustained collaboration in support of the curriculum. The school decided to use pupil enthusiasm for space and astronomy as a way of increasing take-up of GCSE and A-level Physics, and worked with academics at the university to put together a comprehensive new programme, including new resources, joint teaching of the A-level Physics "Astrophysics" module, and visits to UCL's Mill Hill Observatory. UCL has also worked with the school on the development of the "Further Physics: observing the universe" module. UCL has worked as much with the school's teachers as with their pupils, supporting them with subject knowledge and in their work with technical data. Here again, as with the Imperial College / Villiers School Partnership, complementarity of expertise is crucial to the partnership, and highlights just how effective this kind of collaboration can be: between 2005 and 2008, student take-up of Physics GCSE had risen from 15 to 108, with the percentage of students achieving 2 GCSE A*-C grades in science rising from 46% to 62%. The numbers studying A-level Physics have also risen significantly. Furthermore, Alexandra Park School has now been designated one of a national network of 30 Capital Space Schools with funding from the Science and Technology Funding Council, through the Specialist Schools and Academies Trust (SSAT).

A third example demonstrates the ways in which pupils' experience of research can have a positive impact on their attainment in school, and their perceptions of a particular subject. The London School of Hygiene and Tropical Medicine (LSHTM) worked with pupils from schools in the London Borough of Barking and Dagenham to provide them with work experience placements as trainee researchers and scientists. These "trainees" were given the chance to undertake genuine research into the link between deprivation and health, drawing on their experiences in their own communities. The programme has now developed to include research on a wider range of global health issues, and pupils are supported to develop their own research ideas, and to present their findings to internal academic seminars. They have even presented to representatives of the World Health Organisation. There are significant benefits to all involved, with the pupils experiencing the excitement and satisfaction of the intellectual challenge of working with scientists and being encouraged to ask questions and develop independence of thought, as well as gaining in confidence as they learn that eminent scientists genuinely have respect for their questions and ideas. The school and the Local Authority have greatly benefited in that well over 300 pupils have been involved and their GCSE Science grades have improved by a grade or more than was predicted; furthermore, 50% of the original cohort are now studying medicine and science subjects at university.

Schools and universities are now recognising the importance of continuing to innovate in pedagogy, both in our own spheres and together, and these examples demonstrate just how powerful and effective a collaborative approach can be. At the same time, such innovation is most successful where both sectors take a "hands-on", real world approach to teaching and learning. Each of these projects has sought to do more than just impart knowledge or enrich an existing curriculum; they are also about training pupils to recognise the importance of generic and subject-specific skills – including the practical application of theoretical knowledge; presentation skills; research skills and an understanding of what it means to work as a professional in a particular field. Institutions at secondary and tertiary level must begin to include in our curricula more explicit opportunities for our students to develop such skills. For too long, skills development has been associated with "vocational" subjects, and the research-intensive universities especially have only recently begun to focus on this aspect of education, rehabilitating and re-energising the concept of skills in the context of the needs of our demanding, 21st-century globalised world.

One of the problems with the English secondary school system is the ongoing commitment to specialisation in the move up from GCSE to AS to A2 qualifications, whereas employers and national economies in the 21st-century will above all need people who are able to think across discipline boundaries, make connections, and seek solutions through interdisciplinary thinking. This is why it is vital that schools and universities work together in offering, wherever possible, engagement with ground-breaking research and workplace experience, as well as working with other initiatives such as supplementary schools, the Languages Ladder, and so on.

The increase in skills development, especially in the research-intensive universities, does not come from any instrumentalist imperative. Rather, it is generated by a recognition that it is no longer enough to satisfy ourselves that our students have assimilated and can use knowledge and understanding of a particular discipline or disciplines and by an awareness of the importance of specifically linking the ethos and vision of our individual universities to the creation of particular types of graduates.

This is resulting in some universities moving away from the traditional single honours degree towards more generic and/or interdisciplinary degrees. One of the best known examples is the "Melbourne Model" developed by the University of Melbourne, Australia. At the core of this Model are six "new generation" degrees, which combine depth in one or more disciplines with breadth of studies and workplace experience.[2] In this Model, it is precisely the breadth which is the defining feature, and the Melbourne vision is predicated on the belief that by studying up to 25% of their degree programmes from areas other than their chosen core disciplines, their students will develop a wide range of skills, expand the frontiers of their knowledge and learn new ways of thinking about issues and problems.

At UCL, we have been moving increasingly to generic degrees, such as BSc in Biomedical Sciences, BSc in Human Sciences, BSc in Natural Sciences, etc. We are also currently developing a special UK/UCL version of a liberal arts degree which will be a highly interdisciplinary degree (in a sense a BA-BSc), and students will need at least one science A2 Level and one humanities A2 Level of their 3 A Levels to gain entry to it. Unlike the US liberal arts degrees, it will have a series of pathways to which students will apply (Health; Sciences; Cultures). It will be a 4-year programme, with core courses in the 1st and 2nd year, and students will also choose optional courses appropriate to their chosen pathway. The 3rd year will be spent either abroad studying, volunteering or on a work placement or in the UK on a work placement or an internship.

Furthermore, at UCL, we seek to realise our pedagogic vision through our framework for Education for Global Citizenship.[3] Our aim is to produce graduates who are critical and creative thinkers; who are ambitious, but also idealistic and committed to ethical behaviour; who are aware of the intellectual and social value of cultural difference; who are entrepreneurs with the ability to innovate; who are willing to assume leadership roles (in the family, the community and the work place); and who are highly employable and ready to embrace professional mobility.

Underpinning our educational vision at UCL is a passionate belief in the importance of communicating to and exploring with our students the importance of the context within which their learning and researches take place and will be useful. This global vision is central also to our vision for the UCL Academy which we are sponsoring and which will open in 2011. Of course, in some schools, there is an heightened awareness of the need in today's world to offer pupils a wider and more challenging context within which to think and to learn. One of the best examples of this is the Perspectives on Science (PoS) course, which has at its heart a commitment to contextualising learning and to ensuring that that pupils focus on a research question of their own choosing. PoS offers an excellent model for the Extended Project Qualification courses

---

[2] http://www.futurestudents.unimelb.edu.au/melbournemodel.html (last accessed 24th January 2010).

[3] http://www.ucl.ac.uk/global_citizenship/ (last accessed 24th January 2010).

and is leading to further Capital Perspectives approaches, such as "Culture and Identity" and "People, Power and Wealth".[4]

Significantly, as we at UCL developed our educational vision for the Academy that we are sponsoring in Camden (to open in 2011) and as we develop the core courses for our "liberal arts" degree, we have been influenced by what we have seen of PoS both in the course materials and in the classrooms at Rugby School. It is this kind of dynamic and ongoing cross-fertilisation between sectors which will underpin and enable the holistic approach to education that will best prepare our young people for their future lives and careers.

The two aspects which must surely dominate curricular thinking over the next few decades are (a) how to ensure that both knowledge and the learning process are consistently contextualised and (b) how to ensure that research (in all subjects) is at the heart of the learning experience of secondary and tertiary level students.

If we are honest, the relationship between universities and schools still usually takes the form of the now traditional Widening Participation or Outreach activities: "enrichment" or "enhancement". These are, of course, admirable activities: what could be more important than raising the aspirations of our young people or helping pupils and their teachers to think more deeply and more creatively about Physics or Philosophy or whatever? Nonetheless, we need to admit that there is very little real curriculum discussion between schools and universities. All too often I have heard complaints that students are coming up with the "wrong" kind of Maths training or the "wrong" kind of preparation in English or Modern Languages, for example. The result of this is that universities often put on (excellent) remedial or "bridging" courses in, say, Maths, give intensive courses in French grammar, or train students quickly in reading and analysing an entire novel in a couple of weeks. This is, however, essentially ignoring the real problem which is that there is little sustained curriculum discussion between universities and schools and/or curriculum and exam authorities. Universities need to engage more pro-actively with the schools with which they work and must learn to learn from them. Universities must also engage more with each other, with the various Subject Associations and with the school curriculum authorities in order to identify and articulate shared visions of how we can work together to achieve shared outcomes for our young people.

Through our work with schools and through our public engagement work, we in the UK universities are now learning genuinely how to listen and how to allow school pupils and members of the public not only to challenge our ideas

---

[4] For further details of Perspectives on Science and similar courses, see 'The Perspectives Model for the EPQ' in this volume, pp. 49-53.

and question the significance of our discoveries, but also to contribute to the knowledge which we are interrogating or even creating. And we now recognise explicitly that, through our various processes of communicating and working with secondary pupils and their teachers, we gain new perspectives and are offered new pathways forward in thinking about our discoveries as well as new insights on pedagogy for the 21st century. Crucially, we are learning gradually to undo decades, even centuries, of assumptions about how and where knowledge is created and by whom. We are also learning to interrogate notions of ownership of knowledge and assumptions about who is interested in knowledge and why.

Hierarchies of learning are enshrined by the very lexicon of our traditional UK taxonomic language of "primary, secondary, tertiary (or further/higher) education". Language is indeed power, and as such it often fossilises positions of power and esteem. Yet hierarchies are neither appropriate nor useful in education. We all, in our various sectors and from our various institutional standpoints, need to work together to create in the UK the best learning environment possible, seeking actively to learn from each other as we educate our students. Much has been achieved, but so much more can – and must – be done. We may even move from linear rhetorics and visions of "Education, Education, Education" to a holistic or, perhaps even better, to an actively circular conception of how education operates pedagogically, philosophically – and politically.

LIBERATING LEARNING, LIBERAL EDUCATION

AC Grayling

Consider the desired outcomes respectively of education and training. The result of an education should be a desire and an ability to keep on learning and to benefit from what one thus learns; the result of a training should be possession of a well-functioning skill. Schools and universities are in the business of mixing education and training in different proportions, depending on the subject matter; but each has a distinctive content and aim.

From the basic skills of numeracy and literacy, in which young children should be trained to the point of automatic mastery of times tables, spelling and grammar, to the vocational skills required in engineering, surgery, accountancy, and more, *training* is the essence.

For an ability to acquire and evaluate information, to think critically and deeply, to draw rational inferences, to apply knowledge and what is more than knowledge, namely understanding and insight, one needs *education*. This is what is meant by saying that the outcome of education should be a continuing desire and ability to learn and to benefit from what one learns.

Now it is evident that education and training are mutually dependent and reinforcing aspects of the process we habitually lump under the name "education", because an education is not possible without training in basic skills, and vocational training of almost all kinds is most successful when conjoined with the capacities and potentials provided by education. But, in general tendency, where training is directed towards a profession or at least saleable skill in the job market, education is far more than this. Its benefits of course apply in the job market too, but they also apply in every other aspect of life. Aristotle said, "We educate ourselves so that we can make a noble use of our leisure," a wonderfully classical view of what the capacities that a schooling of the intellectual powers and the emotional sensibilities is for.

Aristotle's dictum is indeed richly suggestive, and when it comes to considering education as such – the process of equipping people to learn and to benefit from what they learn – one does well to keep it at the forefront of attention. For when it is there, it is a constant reminder that education is for the person, not merely the employee; it is for the possibility of there being a reflective voter, a thinking friend, a considerate father, a good lover, an engaged citizen, a reader, an interested participant in the conversation of mankind and its hopes for progress, all in one and the same individual.

This sounds utopian, but so be it: Wilde rightly pointed out that the map of the world each of us carries in his head must have Utopia on it, and in education nothing short of the ideal should be the ideal. Alas, though, this conception of education involves what is its own chief obstacle. The key to it is the autonomy of the educand, not merely in the sense that he or she is a self-determining individual, but in the sense that he or she is ultimately responsible for the educational process. To be fully educated, in other words, we must educate ourselves. The problem is a familiar enough one; the young are not always clear about the value of doing the work required. In our desire to impart as much information and capacity as we can to our pupils, we tempt ourselves into doing too much for them: we seek ways of making things easier, of shedding the roughage, eventually of spoon-feeding. I see this in the lengthy and careful bullet-pointed lecture handouts of colleagues, in the appalling practice of selections from texts instead of whole texts, in the fare that has been through the pabulising blender of a certain kind of simplifying, over-organising "educational" technology.

Pupils can be helped, certainly; guidance from those who have trodden the path before them, guidance about worthwhile reading, challenge and questioning, a demand to be clearer, more accurate, to give reasons for their conclusions and to ensure that they are good reasons – all this is what teachers, tutors, guides can provide. But the work of becoming a lifelong learner, thinker and evaluator can of course only be done by the educand. I tell my pupils at the beginning of a lecture course to consider the following: that if at the end of a lecture I required them to remain in their seats and to listen to the same lecture again, they would be restive and bored because they have just heard it all. But if at the end of a lecture I asked them to stand up and deliver the lecture they have just heard, they would not be able to do it. Why not? Because sitting and listening yields at best passive knowledge; giving the lecture requires active knowledge. And the latter only comes from seeking, reading, writing, discussing, reflecting, through which one makes the knowledge one's own, thereby shaping it into something that truly lies at one's disposal.

As this example implies, knowledge as such is not yet the point of an education, though certainly it is a central part of it. The stage beyond knowledge is understanding – and this is the stage that really counts. Understanding what you know is what makes it genuinely usable. It stands at the level of insight and effectiveness. It is as far beyond knowledge as knowledge is beyond mere data. To turn data into knowledge, the data have to be ordered and arranged; to understand what one knows, one has to have worked with the knowledge, applied it, tested it in the practice of reasoning and debate. To produce the sort of person who has such understanding is the goal of education.

The other factor – that education should result in individuals who keep on educating themselves all their lives long, who feel the necessity to do so and relish it – is a key aspect of outcome. It is far better to equip people with the ability to recognise their ignorance and how to remedy it, than to teach them a list of dates and names. The latter is a strictly finite matter, whereas the former is indefinite: it is an endlessly iterable ability across the whole range, and grows with feeding.

The desideratum that we should mean by "an educated person" the same thing as "a lifelong self-educating person" is greater now than it has ever been, because in the form of the internet we now have a vast store of material available at the touch of a fingertip which the self-educating person can access. I say "material" as opposed to "information" or "data" because these latter expressions carry a connotation of reliability. A great deal of what is on the internet is rubbish, even when it purports to be factual; apart from the barrage of ranting opinion, vituperation, fantasy and smut (I have elsewhere called the internet the largest lavatory wall in history), error is ubiquitous on the internet; it can be and too often is replicated across the internet like a virus, instantly and anonymously. Error need not be malevolently placed there; a single typographical error in a chemical formula, for example, is enough for serious misinformation to be displayed millions of times over, which any number of schoolboys hurrying through their homework might use. This is the purport of saying that to be educated an individual must be good at evaluating information with a critical and informed eye. The word that sums up the ability to assay what one encounters on the internet, in newspapers, in the speeches of politicians and the harangues of tap-room demagogues – indeed everywhere – is: judgment.

There is yet a further aspect to the idea of the educated person: that he or she will be equally well-judging and – yet more – responsive, in social, moral and cultural respects. This indeed is what Aristotle chiefly had in mind: the idea of the cultivated personality. Take as an example what one would, among other things, expect from the literary part of an education. A reflective reading of novels, poems and plays has the potential to offer the reader insights into experiences, characters, ways of life, choices and dilemmas, that he might never encounter in his own personal experience. Further, this insight has the potential to quicken his interest in and acceptance of human variety, and hence to broaden his sympathies. The value of this to the moral life is incalculable. We all like to think we are fairly tolerant, but in fact what we think we tolerate is what we do not really mind. Tolerating others' choices and activities that we dislike, yet which we recognise those others' entitlement to, involves the hard work of genuine tolerance: and success in tolerating depends upon an extension of outlook. Reflective reading is a major aid to personal experience in this.

But for the possibility of moral community more is needed than tolerance. That more is sympathy. There is a fine cliché about how both education and travel "broaden horizons," and like most clichés this one has the merit of truth. Mental horizons are drawn by experience; for the illiterate medieval peasant they coincided with the physical and social horizon of a village, together perhaps with the alarming prescriptive eschatology taught in the local church. Education is a process of multiplying and potentiating experience. It is the provision of many more hooks on which to hang new understandings, new data, new feelings. If there are no hooks for new things to hang upon, they do not stay. To acquire knowledge one has to know things already, both in the sense of "knowledge how" (which training provides) and "knowledge that." In the social and moral case too, therefore, judgment and receptivity are the fruits of education as it should be.

Familiarly, Plato had a metaphysical conception of education as the process of partially reminding people of what they knew – which was everything – in their pre-incarnated existence as pure mind in the Realm of Being, intimate with the eternal Ideas there. A false etymology from Latin "ex" or "e" and "ducere" seems to capture this idea of leading or drawing out what is innate but forgotten in the soul. We talk of eliciting the talents and abilities of our pupils, of bringing to light the potential that lies within them. The contrast is with placing information and skills in previously empty vessels, and it is a good contrast when the focus of attention is nurturing what they already have. "Training" is precisely the right term here; think of a gardener and his vines; the skills presupposed to education and self-education have to exist in order to be fostered. Add to this the direction given towards the bodies of knowledge in the sciences and social sciences, and the resources for education of the sensibilities in the arts and literature, and one sees what the composite process of education has to offer.

One has to conclude with an iteration of the point that, in the end, education is the responsibility of the educand himself or herself. Our institutions of education take the horses to water; we have, in despair at those who will not drink, taken to sloshing the stuff over them. If there is a polemical point in the foregoing, it is that we need to renew efforts at getting them to appreciate the benefits of hydration. For that we need what – the misnomer accordingly understood – we persist in calling "good teachers," dedicated to the task of exhortation and illustration, finding the ends of threads that will lead to the self-educability of the individual, skilled at working with the grain even of the cross-grained character; enthusiastic and dedicated about all that education can do for the quality of lives – such teachers are among the most important people on earth.

THE DECLINE OF HISTORY AND THE FUTURES OF WESTERN CIVILISATION

Niall Ferguson

History matters. Many schoolchildren doubt this. But they are wrong, and they need to be persuaded that they are wrong.

Why does History matter? Well, because there is no such thing as the Future, singular; only futures, plural. There are multiple historical interpretations of History, to be sure, none definitive—but there is only one Past. And although the Past is over, it's important. First, the current world population makes up approximately six per cent of all the human beings who have ever lived. The dead out-number the living, in other words, and we ignore the accumulated experience of such a huge majority of mankind at our peril. Second, the Past is our only reliable guide to the Present and to the multiple futures that lie before us, only one of which will actually happen.

Let us first acknowledge the subject's limitations. Historians are not scientists. They cannot do science in the sense that they can't (and shouldn't even try) to establish universal laws of social or political "physics" with reliable predictive powers. Why? Because there is no possibility of repeating the single, multi-millennium experiment that constitutes the Past. The sample size of human history is one (N=1). Moreover, the "particles" in this one vast experiment have consciousness which is skewed by all kinds of biases. This means that their behaviour is extremely hard to predict. Among the ways that human cognition works is that people have evolved to learn instinctively from their own experience, even if they decline to learn in a more formal way from History. So their behaviour is adaptive. It changes over time.

What historians can do is to analyze and interpret recorded human experience at various different levels ranging from the micro (the individual) to the intermediate (the village, the city, the region) to the macro (the nation state, the empire, the civilisation). They can compare two or more units synchronically or diachronically. They can draw coarse-grained analogies between past and present events—for example, financial crises, revolutions or wars. And, if only for heuristic purposes, they can imagine or simulate alternative "pasts" that did not happen, but might have.

How do historians do these things? First, they commune with the dead by imaginatively reconstructing their experiences. In the words of R. G. Collingwood, "Historical knowledge is the re-enactment of a past thought, incapsulated in a context of present thoughts which, in contradicting it, confine it to a plane different from theirs" (Collingwood 1978: 114). Alternatively, historians can devise "covering laws", in Carl Hempel's sense of general statements about the past that appear to cover most cases, relying more on quantitative data (Hempel 1959). These two modes of historical inquiry allow us to turn the surviving relics of the Past into History – a body of knowledge and interpretation that retrospectively orders and illuminates the human predicament. Any serious predictive statement about the possible futures we may experience is based, implicitly or explicitly, on one or both of these historical procedures. If not, then it belongs in the same category as astrology.

Most intelligent adults, no matter how limited their education, understand that History is important. Even if they have never formally studied the subject, they are quite likely to take an interest in historical subjects. When the television series *Empire: How Britain Made the Modern World* was screened on Channel 4 over six weeks in early 2003, it attracted an average audience of 2.2 million viewers, approximately 10 per cent of all viewers. More than half of all adults in the social category "ABC1" watched the series. More than 200,000 copies of the accompanying book have been sold in the UK alone. Simon Schama's multi-episode series for the BBC, *A History of Britain*, was even more popular. David Starkey has also reached a large proportion of television viewers and readers with his films on the Tudors and other British monarchs. Military historians who have become household names in recent years include Richard Holmes and Anthony Beevor. And journalists such as Peter Snow and Andrew Marr have also been highly successful in reaching a mass audience with historical material.

History, it might be said, has never been more popular. Yet there is a painful paradox. At the very same time, it has never been *less* popular in British schools. History has ceased to be a compulsory part of the British secondary school curriculum after the age of 14, in marked contrast to nearly all other European countries. The most recent statistics for England and Wales indicate the scale of the problem. In 2009 a total of 219,809 candidates sat the GCSE in History, just 4.0 per cent of all GCSEs sat (compared with 4.3% in 1992). More students sat the Design & Technology GCSE (305,809). At A-level the story is worse. There were 49,071 A-level History candidates in 2009, 5.8 per cent of all A-levels sat (down from 6.4 per cent in 1992). More candidates took Psychology (52,872).

Numbers, however, fail to tell the true story of History's decline in British schools. When you consider the content of what is taught to teenagers, you begin to realise that the really surprising thing is how many, not how few, volunteer for the experience of studying the subject. In the space of a generation, History in the sense of a coherent, cumulative narrative covering a significant stretch of time has essentially died in British schools – or been murdered in violent backlash against the traditional "island story" so famously lampooned in Sellar and Yeatman's *1066 and All That*. The result is a complete absence of any meaningful connections between what is taught to students within and between Stage 3, GCSE and A level.

This would be bad enough if the selection of subject matter were merely random. Unfortunately, it is positively and absurdly skewed. Herding behaviour by both teachers and pupils has resulted in the absurd state of affairs that, according to recent data, 51 per cent of GCSE candidates and a staggering 80 per cent of A-level candidates study the history of the Third Reich. As someone who wrote his D.Phil. thesis on inter-war Germany, I yield to no one in my respect for the historiography of Adolf Hitler's rise and fall. But there can be no justification for this excessive focus on the history of a single European country over a period of just a dozen years.

To those outside the teaching profession, the extent to which History as an integral subject has been replaced with a kind of smorgasbord of unrelated "topics" may not be familiar. So it is worth pausing to consider the choices that British teachers and students today confront. At Key Stage 3, students are required to select – from a possible twenty-two – a total of six topics, three of which must be British, two "world" and one European. So far so good. But here is a typical selection:

1. Elizabeth I
2. The British Empire
3. Black Peoples of America
4. Female Suffrage
5. The World Wars
6. The Holocaust

This kind of selection is popular and explains why, when I asked them recently, all three of my children had heard of the Rev. Martin Luther King Jr., but none could tell me anything about Martin Luther.

At GCSE there are a number of different syllabuses. Under OCR A, students study:

1. EITHER: Medicine through Time, OR Crime and Punishment through Time.

2. EITHER: A Modern World Study (relating current events to history), OR A Study in Depth, which needs to be one of the following:

1. Elizabethan England, 1558-1603
2. Britain, 1815-51
3. The American West, 1840-95
4. Germany, c.1919-45
5. South Africa, 1948-c.1995.

In theory a student who has followed the above course at Key Stage 3 would avoid options 1 and 4. But in practice a very large proportion choose either the Tudor option or the Hitler option, since that it was they are already familiar with.

An alternative GCSE course, OCR B, is more traditional. The student covers "International Relations, 1919-1989" – let's start with Hitler, shall we? – followed by a "coursework unit" on one of the following:

1. Germany: The Rise of Hitler
2. Russia: The Bolsheviks, Lenin and Stalin
3. The U.S.A: Boom, Bust and Recovery
4. China under Mao, 1945-c.1976
5. South Africa: The Apartheid State and the Struggle Against It
6. Israel and Her Neighbours, 1945-c.1994

A third GCSE course, Edexcel B, is more focused on British History. The striking point to note here is that, leaving aside the broad "Outline Studies" and the "Coursework Units", the two "Depth Studies" students must undertake are drawn from a list of ten options, none pre-dating 1750 and half including or exclusively covering the twentieth century.

To be fair to those who design the secondary school curriculum, the various A-level courses are somewhat more generous to the medieval and early modern periods. A candidate for OCR AS could opt for a "Document Study" from the period 871-1099, the English History Period 1042-1660, and the European History period 1046-1718. Similar options are available for OCR A2. The obvious question is how many choose these earlier options? The answer is far fewer than study "Appeasement" and "Civil Rights in the U.S.".

The excessive concentration of English and Welsh sixth formers on either Hitler or the Henrys – the Third Reich or the Tudors – was already becoming a cause of concern when I was a College Fellow and Tutor at Oxford in the 1990s. I shudder to think what it must be like to conduct Oxbridge admissions ten years on.

*

Back in 2005, when the Prince of Wales was still striving to change attitudes within the teaching profession, he proposed a number of criteria which might be called the Dartington criteria, after Dartington Manor, where I first came across them. History, he argued, should provide:

1. A sense of continuity and of place
2. Abundant narratives and "maps of the past"
3. A broad range of periods and texts
4. A big picture – but not too big
5. An appreciation of pupils' "cultural inheritance" and "shared past".

At the time, I agreed with most of these. They are certainly a refreshing contrast to what is currently on offer in British classrooms. Now I would like to suggest a way in which they might be fulfilled by a new British History curriculum.

The first step we need to take is to make History compulsory to GCSE. It cannot be wise for British schoolchildren to opt out of historical knowledge and understanding when all their European contemporaries are still studying the subject. Secondly, I recommend that students be examined publicly only twice in four years: at GCSE and A2 level. Thirdly, I believe there should be a mandatory chronological framework over the entire period from Key Stage 3 to GCSE and beyond to AS and A2. All students should cover at least one medieval, one early modern and one modern paper.

The crucial thing, however, is to have something resembling an over-arching story – a meta-narrative, in academic parlance. Here is the one I propose for my new-look History course. It is called *Western Ascendancy*.

Why, you may ask, that word "Western"? Aside from cowboy films, is it not completely *passé*? After all, Stanford University formally abolished the "History of Western Civilisation" as an undergraduate requirement as long ago as 1963, replacing it in 1980 with "Western Culture", then in 1983 with "Cultures, Ideas, and Values" and finally in 1997 with the innocuous "Introduction to the Humanities". And why "Ascendancy", implying as it does some politically incorrect superiority?

19

The answer is simple. Western predominance was a historical reality after around 1500, and certainly after 1800. In that year, Europe and its New World offshoots accounted for 12 per cent of the world's population and (already) around 27 per cent of its total income. By 1913, however, it was 20 per cent of the world's population and more than half – 51 per cent – of the income. Today the West's share is back down to 12 per cent of the population, but still around 45 per cent of the income (Clark 2007). Like it or not, the fact is that after 1500 the world became more Eurocentric. And understanding *why* that happened is the modern historian's biggest challenge.

The great Samuel Johnson summed up the central puzzle of modern History in a passage from his *History of Rasselas: Prince of Abissinia*, published in 1759:

"By what means (said the Prince) are the Europeans thus powerful; or why, since they can so easily visit Asia and Africa for trade or conquest, cannot the Asiaticks and Africans invade their coasts, plant colonies in their ports, and give laws to their natural princes? The same wind that carries them back would bring us thither." – "They are more powerful, Sir, than we, (answered Imlac,) because they are wiser. Knowledge will always predominate over ignorance, as man governs the other animals. But why their knowledge is more than ours, I know not what reason can be given, but the unsearchable will of the Supreme being."

It was indeed surprising. Had you made a tour of the world in the early 1600s you would have hesitated before betting a significant sum that Western Europe would inherit the earth. The challengers for world power were simply so much more impressive.

In 1683 Ottoman Turkey under Mehmed IV (1648-1687) was able to send an army under Grand Vizier Kara Mustafa to besiege – and very nearly conquer – Vienna in 1683. Mughal India in the reign of Shah Jahan (1627-1658) was able to conquer the Deccan and to build the Taj Mahal and the Diwan-i-Am in Delhi. Qing China saw its golden age under the Kangxi Emperor (1662-1722). China had already invented the magnetic compass, paper, gunpowder, the silk reeling frame, the spinning wheel, and the clock. The Muslim world had for many centuries led the West in the crucial field of mathematics. Indian astronomers had been far ahead of their medieval European counterparts.

So why did the states of Western Europe – Portugal, Spain, France, the Netherlands and Britain – end up trouncing all these Eastern competitors not only economically but also militarily and in some respects also culturally, so that by 1900 the world very clearly was dominated by a club of Western empires. The great anthropologist Jared Diamond's answer to this question is essentially:

geography, which determined two very different political orders. In the great plains of Eastern Eurasia, monolithic Oriental empires evolved which had the fatal ability to stifle innovation – banning Chinese oceanic voyages after 1432, for example. In mountainous, river-divided Western Eurasia, by contrast, multiple monarchies and city-states engaged in creative competition and communication, and it was these processes that accelerated innovation sufficiently for an industrial revolution, eventually, to take place (Diamond 1999). The argument is almost irresistibly attractive, but for one small difficulty. From the vantage point of the 1630s and 1640s, political fragmentation in Europe meant civil war and chaos.

Other hypotheses exist. According to Pomeranz (2000) it was the acquisition of colonial "ghost acres" and the fortunate location of European coal deposits that gave the West the edge over the East. According to Landes (1998) it was the cultural legacies of the Reformation. North (2005) emphasises the role of economic and political institutions. There is no definitive answer and nor does one seem likely to emerge. But that the question is the right one seems clear.

The pedagogical value of seeking to explain Western ascendancy is twofold. First, it provides a clear meta-narrative for around five hundred years of world history. Secondly, it makes a comparative approach to History unavoidable, for clearly an interpretation of Western success requires some complementary explanation of Eastern stagnation. Thirdly, understanding Western ascendancy encourages students to re-examine the present and to address the related question about the future, namely: Are we approaching the end of Western ascendancy?

If I had to construct a new core curriculum for British schoolchildren studying History, I would structure it around six key questions:

1. What was the role of institutions (as against resource endowments) in the "great divergence" of the West from the East after 1500?
2. Why was there no Scientific Revolution outside the West?
3. Why did Western polities make the transition to truly representative governments before others?
4. How far was Western ascendancy due to imperial exploitation and coercion?
5. Why did the Industrial Revolution and the Consumer Society originate in the West?
6. Did religion (e.g. Weber's "Protestant ethic") play any significant role in Western ascendancy?

I do not yet claim to have conclusive answers to these questions, but if I were permitted to hazard some hypotheses they would go as follows. There were, in essence, six "killer applications" that allowed the West to establish a dominant role over the Western world:

1. Market capitalism
2. The scientific method
3. The common law and representative government
4. The idea of a liberal empire
5. The consumer society
6. The Protestant work ethic

How far the West can any longer claim to monopolise these six things is a matter for debate. What is certain is that most of them have been more or less successfully replicated in at least some major non-Western societies.

*

This sketch for a new History curriculum has one obvious flaw. It does not extend backwards to cover the first era of Western ascendancy in the ancient world, nor does it enable to students to study the decline of Western civilization that followed the sack of Rome. However, at least some of that historical knowledge can be acquired by the study of what remains of Classics. Courses in Greek and Roman language and civilization offer an ideal complement to the history of what might be called "Western Civilisation 2.0" after 1500.

Let me not be misinterpreted. This is not an attempt to turn the clock back. The point of studying Western ascendancy is not to slip some covert imperial apologia into the secondary school curriculum. On the contrary, the great strength of this framework is that it allows students to study world history without falling into the trap of relativism, i.e. arguing as if the Ashanti Empire were in some way the equal of the British Empire. Western ascendancy was not all good, any more than it was all bad. It was simply what happened and, of all the things that happened over the past five centuries, the thing that changed the world the most. That so few British schoolchildren are even aware of this is deplorable. Knowing the names of Henry VIII's six wives or the date of the Reichstag fire is no substitute for having a real historical education.

We have recently witnessed a successful campaign to improve the quality of food served for lunch in British schools. It is time for an equivalent campaign against Junk History.

BIBLIOGRAPHY

Clark, G. (2007) A *Farewell to Alms: A Brief Economic History of the World*. Princeton: Princeton University Press.

Collingwood, R.G. (1978) *An Autobiography*. Oxford: Clarendon Press

Diamond, J. (1999), *How to Get Rich*. Edge. 56.

Hempel, C. (1959) "The Function of General Laws in History", in Patrick Gardiner (ed.), *Theories of History. Glencoe*, Illinois/London: 344-55.

Landes, D.S. (1998) *The Wealth and Poverty of Nations: Why Some are So Rich and Some So Poor*. New York: W.W. Norton.

North, D.C. (2005) *Understanding the Process of Economic Change*. Princeton: Princeton University Press.

Pomeranz, K. (2000) *The Great Divergence: China, Europe and the Making of the Modern World Economy*. Princeton: Princeton University Press.

SCIENCE, HISTORY, AND PHILOSOPHY

Simon Blackburn

When she was in her teens my daughter came home from her school—one of the country's best High Schools for girls—and announced that she was through with science. I said that was a pity, and asked why. It turned out that they had been "learning the pendulum", and this consisted, apparently, in solving for velocity at the bottom of the swing using the equation of potential energy at the top and kinetic energy at the bottom. I asked what was the problem, and she said she didn't understand what this thing "energy" was, that was the same throughout: there was nothing she could see that stayed the same about the bob at the top and bottom of its swing. I asked if she had put her problem to the teacher. Yes. And what did she say? "Get on and solve the equation".

Now the concept of energy in question arrived in science some two centuries after Galileo's groundbreaking investigation of the pendulum, and only after the need for the concept in thermodynamics had made itself felt. One of the first uses of the phrases "kinetic energy" and "potential energy" was in Thomson & Tait's *Elements of Natural Philosophy*, produced as late as 1873. During the previous two centuries not only Galileo, but Descartes, Huygens, Euler and many others had refined the mathematics and physics of the pendulum in countless fascinating ways. Some of this effort was motivated by commercial and nautical needs connected with the expansion of Europe and the link between navigation and chronometry. I do not know the best way to excite a young person's mind with the drama of this story. But I am sure that it is not by telling them to "get on and solve the equation".

I do not blame the teacher: she may have been anxious about meeting some targets set by politicians and civil servants who themselves knew no better. Examinations are easier to set and much, much, easier to mark if all that has to be done is to put down a figure for a velocity rather than exhibit any kind of understanding of the thought processes of those who painfully and slowly, piecemeal and controversially, stumbled towards the understandings we have. The children who excel at it could doubtless, in other circumstances, equally have excelled at learning the Koran by heart.

Yet – whoever cared a fig about the velocity of a pendulum at the bottom of its swing? The thing that mattered about pendula was their isochronous oscillation and the uses Europe could make of that.

Science taught as it was to my daughter deserves to see imaginative and good minds avoiding it like the plague. It is also disturbing to think of the simulacrum of understanding that the children who could put up with it must have. They can solve the equation, and no doubt pass the exams, but what do they thereby understand of the classical conception of energy? I know from my own history that when I arrived in Cambridge having passed the entrance in Natural Sciences, I understood almost nothing of the mathematics and physics underlying the examination hoops that I had jumped through without too much difficulty. It was only after changing to philosophy, and when I came, for instance, to read the history of the concept of a limit in classical mathematics, that I began to see the calculus as anything more than a mathematical trick. I believe that Russell's *Introduction to Mathematical Philosophy* and Nagel's empiricist classic *The Structure of Science* taught me more in a vacation's reading than three years of mathematics and physics at school had done.

The historian and philosopher R. G. Collingwood held that to understand a piece of history you had to think as the agents of the time did. You have to re-enact their thoughts for yourself, in your own voice, as it were. I think if my daughter had been led to re-enact Galileo's discovery of the isochronous swing of the pendulum – or Descartes's disbelief in it on good empirical grounds – or the harnessing of the pendulum to clocks by the invention of an escape mechanism – or Huygens's cycloidal modification – or how subsequent mathematicians developed the ideas leading to $T = 2\pi\sqrt{L/g}$ – then something of the romance of science, and an appreciation of the sheer magnitude of its achievements, would have resulted.[1]

I also think such an education would be liberating in a larger way. Liberation requires not taking for granted things that we are told to take for granted, or that familiarity and lack of imagination make us take for granted. If students think of science as a vast repository of fact on the top of which we fortunately sit, then they are being encouraged to take too much for granted. The habit of challenge and inquiry dries up, and science itself suffers. Science is not distinguished because of how much scientists know, but because of the habits of questioning, hypothesizing, falsifying, and theory building that make up its activities. To count as scientifically educated students, in short, need to understand science as

---

[1] The history of the pendulum is well told by the educational writer Michael Matthews, *Time for Science Education*, Kluwer, 2000.

process rather than as product. Quizzing them on its products is surely a very doubtful way to turn them into participants in the process.

It is not just the educational system that fails to recognize this. I think there are forces within the scientific community itself which want to advertise the product rather than the procedures, just as conjurors want to show you the trick rather than how it is done. Authority and power go with mystique. But there is a cost to that, for a small glimpse of the process may then be enough to disenchant the bewildered public. We are no longer surprised that much of what is presented as research in clinical pharmacology is warped by the presence of money, so that trials funded by drug companies are systematically more positive about the effects of their drugs than independent trials are. Here cautious scepticism is in order.

In a similar way, many people have been galvanized to scepticism about the science of measurement of the earth's temperature since the embarrassing emails from the University of East Anglia were brought to light. But I suggest that we were only surprised by those because we had been led to believe that science is some kind of missile infallibly guided towards the truth, instead of a boat tacking here and there under the guidance of a not very harmonious crew partly gripped by ordinary historical processes of human ambition, greed, rivalry, and pig-headedness in all their full carnival colours. It is not too difficult to suspect that these traits are behind what we might call the religious aspect of global warming panic; it is too early to say to what extent they lie behind the science.

For a different kind of example, a fascinating educational opportunity is afforded by the global financial collapse of 2008. Some banks now nationalized or bailed out are said to have employed up to 4000 highly-paid, highly educated "risk analysts". No doubt some of them saw that things were getting out of hand, but none of them stopped crunching the formulae and methods that assured them that all was well. The philosophy of probability might just have helped: from Hume onwards philosophers have known that there is no unique "probability space" within which the most everyday probabilities (the probability of the sun rising tomorrow, for instance) can be calculated. The mathematicians forgot that prices do not take independent random walks: what Keynes called the "animal spirits" of agents in a stockmarket are contagious and interdependent. And this means that what might look to be a minimal risk, for instance of all prices heading downwards simultaneously, may turn out to be a very large one. The mathematicians who ended up bleating about a "one-in-ten-thousand-year" event were illustrating their own poor understandings rather than the perversity of nature.

An understanding of the philosophy would surely have been worth an hour or two out of the time those 4000 mathematicians spent mastering the theology of the Black-Scholes formula or the infallibility of Monte Carlo methods. Of course, it is easy to be wise after the event, but it has to be worth asking whether people could have been wiser before the event: after all as long ago as 1841, in the book that introduced the phrase "the madness of crowds" the author Charles Mackay used financial bubbles as one of his main examples.[2]

It is not easy to sell philosophy and history to government: the Arts and Humanities Research Council receives only 4% of the money allocated to (civilian) research by the unfortunately named Department of Business, Innovation, and Skills. The Confederation of British Industry likes scientists and engineers, but this is largely because with a greater supply of scientists and engineers than is needed to meet demand, industry can keep down the current low price they pay for their expertise. There are few political policies about which it is unwise to ask: "cui bono?"

We all have a stake in the skills of scientists and engineers. But we also have a stake in their own understanding of their own sciences, and that should include an understanding of the human forces that shape science. We should not be surprised that myopic educations produce myopic specialists. And the world is too full of surprises, and may be full of bigger ones in quite a near future, for us to be happy with any education that does not leave people imaginative, open, and alert to as many of the human and natural phenomena that surround them, and that brought them to where they are now, as they can possibly be.

---

[2] Charles Mackay, *Extraordinary Popular Delusions and the Madness of Crowds.*

PROMOTING ENGAGEMENT WITH SCIENCE EDUCATION

Michael Reiss

Most 11 year-olds start their secondary education keen to learn science. The excitement of experiments in chemistry and other science subjects in real laboratories is keenly anticipated. Why then are most 16 year-olds in the UK delighted to give up science as soon as they have finished their GCSEs or Scottish Highers (Reiss 2000; Schreiner 2006)?

There are three main reasons. The first is that most teaching of school science doesn't take enough account of *how* people learn about science nowadays. The second is that the science curriculum doesn't take enough account of *what* young people want to learn about. The third is that we have got ourselves into a situation where many science teachers are *too constrained* in what they can teach.

School science doesn't usually take enough account of *how* people learn science

Let's start with the problem that school science doesn't usually take enough account of how people learn science. Gone are the days when it was quite exciting to do an experiment in a school science lab to show that plants make starch or that copper gains in mass when it burns. Nowadays, all of us are bombarded with science stories in the media 24 hours a day. If I just spend a minute looking at the BBC News website as I write this (20 December 2009) I find excellent accounts of the following stories:

- Member-states of the European Space Agency have given final approval to revised plans to explore Mars.
- The discovery of a fossilised skeleton that has become a "central character in the story of human evolution" has been named the science breakthrough of 2009.
- Scientists say they have made a synthetic blood-clotting agent that could help wounded troops and patients.

In other words, just one minute on the net results in a lot of interesting and absolutely up-to-date science. Indeed, the opportunities for me to access contemporary science are apparently endless. I can look digitally through telescopes giving me live views of far-off galaxies and through web-cams that show me endangered birds of prey feeding their young in real time. How can schools compete?

We need to acknowledge that much of where today's young people will learn about science will not be in the classroom but via such as extra-school sources as the internet, science museums, television, radio, magazines and science centres. This is not, of course, to imply that there isn't a central place for school science lessons. There is. School science lessons can provide a number of ways of learning that are far less available elsewhere:

- School science lessons provide opportunities for specialist and highly qualified teachers of science to structure classroom dialogue. When I attempt to teach the particle theory of matter or the process of photosynthesis, I do with a detailed knowledge of the misconceptions that learners typically have. Such knowledge is the result partly of my own teaching experience and partly of time spent listening to other science teachers and educators and reading what they have written.
- School science lessons provide opportunities for hands-on practical work and for students to learn from teacher demonstrations. We have a wonderful tradition in the UK of such practical work but the last couple of decades have almost certainly seen a narrowing of the sorts of practical work that students experience. I welcome the current "Getting Practical" initiative that is being undertaken by the Association for Science Education and others (ASE 2009). This is a project designed to help teachers to improve the following:

  o Clarity of the learning outcomes associated with practical work.
  o Effectiveness and impact of the practical work.
  o Sustainability of this approach for ongoing improvements.
  o Quality rather than quantity of practical work used.

The science curriculum doesn't take enough account of *what* young people want to learn about

School science needs to take more account of what students want to learn. At present the government dictates that all 11-16 year-olds in state schools have to learn equal amounts of biology, chemistry and physics – and you get only a limited choice about what you learn in those subjects. I am in favour of 11-16 year-olds having more control over what they study. In certain respects the 2006 changes to the science curriculum at GCSE were a move in that direction and, if it ever sees the light of day, the Science Diploma has the potential to contribute in this respect too by catering for a group of young people who, especially post-16, are not well served at present.

A few years ago I carried out a study with colleagues called "The Student Review of the Science Curriculum" (Cerini et al 2003). Over 350 students, aged 16-19, designed possible questions for a web-based questionnaire at regional meetings held across England. In the six weeks to 8th February 2002, a total of 1500 questionnaires were submitted.

Analysis of these responses showed considerable student dissatisfaction with the science curriculum. The students came up with ten recommendations:

1. *Ethical and controversial issues*
   The science curriculum should include more ethical and controversial issues. These should not be hived off into occasional discrete topics but included throughout the curriculum.
2. *Practical work*
   Practical work should be strongly encouraged and relevant to the syllabus. The practicals need to be supervised, they need to work and they need up-to-date equipment.
3. *Dissection*
   Schools should provide students with the opportunity to do dissection but individual students should have the choice as to whether or not they do dissection.
4. *Science and maths*
   The fundamentals of maths should be covered in maths lessons but science lessons should explicitly include a coherent treatment of the maths needed for science. Better communication is needed between science and maths teachers.
5. *Science teachers*
   Good science teachers are crucial. Science teachers should be qualified to teach science and should have the appropriate subject specialism within science, if possible.
6. *Slimming the curriculum*
   The science curriculum should cover fewer topics to allow for more in-depth treatment and for more detailed explanations.
7. *Discussions in science*
   There should be more discussions in science classes. Discussions provide students with the opportunity to learn from someone other than

their teacher and, healthily, to disagree with teachers and develop their own ideas.

8. *Good science teaching*

Learning is helped by having a teacher who can engage with students and by the use of visually stimulating material.

9. *Making chemistry and physics more popular*

The popularity of chemistry and physics would be raised if they connected more with real-life situations, as biology does, and included more ethical issues.

10. *Primary science*

In primary school, integration between science and other subjects is important. Primary science should be placed at the same level of importance as English and maths. Better equipment is needed for primary science teaching.

I am not claiming that every one of these ten recommendations should immediately be implemented. But I am saying that many of them should be and that those who put together school science curricula need to take more account of what 11-16 year-olds want to learn.

Many science teachers are *too constrained* in what they can teach

Educational research is increasingly showing what most students, teachers and parents have long known. What matters more than just about anything in determining how well a student learns is the quality of the teaching they receive (Hattie 2009). Too much of politicians' time, effort and money in education is directed at changing the structures of education (eg, the types of schools we have), the organisation of schools or the curriculum, important though the curriculum is. Students would learn more if we gave more opportunities – as some other countries do and the UK independent sector is more able than the state sector to do – for teachers to concentrate on teaching well.

In the UK, particularly in England, science teachers are constrained by a number of factors. For a start, in common with teachers of all subjects, they, particularly in the state sector, are bombarded with government requirements and subject to an inspection regime that gives too much emphasis to a narrow conceptualisation of education, as revealed by raw examination results, and too little emphasis to a broader understanding, including engagement with learning as manifested by a wish to continue to study. To be fair, while I fear that Ofsted's views about education are becoming ever more narrow, some progress has been made by government in regard to reducing the barriers to taking students on field trips and other extra-school excursions. Such extra-school learning activities are particularly important in science as they enable rich connections to be made between the science that is learnt in a school laboratory (where a simplified and stripped down version of nature is presented) and the science that can be learnt in the "real world" (Braund & Reiss 2004).

But perhaps the most important constraint – and one that would cost little in time or money to ameliorate – is that of assessment. As a recent major and well researched report by a House of Commons Select Committee put it:

> "… in recent years the Government has emphasised central control of the education system through testing and associated targets and performance tables, placing test results in a new and more complex context with wide-ranging consequences … we find that the use of national test results for the purpose of school accountability has resulted in some schools emphasising the maximisation of test results at the expense of a more rounded education for their pupils … A variety of classroom practices aimed at improving test results has distorted the education of some children, which may leave them unprepared for higher education and employment. We find that "teaching to the test" and narrowing of the taught curriculum are widespread phenomena in schools … Tests, however, can only test a limited range of the skills and activities which are properly part of a rounded education, so that a focus on improving test results compromises teachers' creativity in the classroom and children's access to a balanced curriculum."

House of Commons Children, Schools and Families Committee (2008: 3)

Conclusion

Science is a fascinating subject. It can help us understand how stars are born and how they die, why some bacteria can reproduce every 20 minutes whereas some trees live over a thousand years. It can give us the technology to help us live longer, healthier lives and to find alternatives to fossil fuels. It helps us to see ourselves in a new light. But we need to reform the science that is taught in schools and how it is taught and examined, otherwise not enough people will want to study science post-16, let alone go into it for a career.

BIBLIOGRAPHY

ASE (2009) Getting Practical – Improving Practical Work in Science Programme.
http://www.schoolscience.co.uk/search.cfm?FaArea1=customWidgets.cont entItem_show_1&cit_id=4578&&subject_id= (last accessed December 20th 2009).

Braund, M. & Reiss, M. J. (Eds) (2004) *Learning Science Outside the Classroom*. London: RoutledgeFalmer.

Cerini, B., Murray, I. & Reiss, M. (2003) *Student Review of the Science Curriculum: Major Findings*. London: Planet Science. Available at http://www.planet-science.com/sciteach/review/Findings.pdf (last accessed December 20th 2009).

Hattie, J. A. C. (2009) *Visible Learning: A Synthesis of over 800 Meta-analyses Relating to Achievement*. Abingdon: Routledge.

House of Commons Children, Schools and Families Committee (2008) *Testing and Assessment: Third Report of Session 2007–08 Volume I*. London: House of Commons. Available at http://www.parliament.the-stationery-office.co.uk/pa/cm200708/cmselect/cmchilsch/169/169.pdf (last accessed December 20th 2009).

Reiss, M. J. (2000) *Understanding Science Lessons: Five Years of Science Teaching*. Buckingham: Open University Press.

Schreiner, C. (2006) Exploring a ROSE-garden: Norwegian Youth's Orientations towards Science – Seen as Signs of Late Modern Identities. Doctoral thesis. Oslo: University of Oslo, Faculty of Education.

LEARNING AND CONTROL: TOWARDS AN IMPROVED MODEL FOR CURRICULUM DEVELOPMENT

Simon Lebus

It is hard to imagine a present-day Secretary of State for Education proclaiming, as Ken Clarke did in 1991, that "My writ does not run in any serious respect over the day-to-day organisation of a solitary education establishment in the country.... The day-to-day management of schools is not within my responsibility".[1] Since then there has been a seemingly unstoppable extension of central control. This was well illustrated recently when the TES reported that School Principals receive almost 4,000 pages of e-mailed Government guidance a year – 1,269,000 words in the twelve months between April 2008 and 2009.[2]

At the same time, public spending on education between 1987 and 2008 doubled from £41.3 to £83 billion,[3] while more than a quarter of the English population is now in education or training,[4] and the proportion of 18-30 year olds in HE is up from around 20% in 1980 to its present level of approximately 43%.[5]

However, it is not straightforward to calculate the educational benefit. Public exam results, in principle one of the clearest measures of achievement, have become a discredited currency as a result of anxieties about dumbing down and an apparently relentless rise in the number of students securing top grades.

---

[1] Education, Science and Arts Select Committee, "Standards of Reading in Primary Schools" HC (1990-91) 268-ii [178].

[2] William Stewart, "School management: Tories claim DCSF 'swamp' schools with guidance", http://www.tes.co.uk/article.aspx?storycode=6020400 (accessed August 14th 2009).

[3] Paul Bolton, "Education spending in the UK",
http://www.parliament.uk/commons/lib/research/briefings/snsg-01078.pdf (accessed April 22nd 2009).

[4] Sean Coughlan, "'One in four' people in education",
http://news.bbc.co.uk/1/hi/education/8353257.stm (accessed December 1st 2009)

[5] http://www.dcsf.gov.uk/rsgateway/DB/SFR/s000839/SFR02-2009appendix.pdf (accessed December 6th 2009).

Scores of three As in A-levels, for example, have more than doubled over the last fifteen years to the present level of 17%[6] and universities protest that they are unable to differentiate students at the top end of the ability range – though many of them, worried about access, are now refusing to use the A* grade introduced precisely to help them do so.

Employers too complain. In one six-week period in late 2009, Sir Stuart Rose of Marks & Spencer claimed of school leavers that: "They cannot do reading. They cannot do arithmetic. They cannot do writing."[7] While Sir Terry Leahy of Tesco (and a former member of the National Council of Educational Excellence) described standards in schools as "woefully low",[8] and Sir Michael Rake, Chairman of British Telecom, called for the scrapping of A-levels and GCSEs.[9]

This is all of a piece with the well-established and now almost ritual discourse about standards that takes place at exam results time every August. More troubling, though, are studies of young people's cognitive capacity. Professor James Flynn, responsible for identifying the Flynn effect whereby IQ scores of successive generations in industrialised countries have risen over the last hundred or so years, carried out tests in 2008 suggesting that the IQ score of an average 14 year old dropped by more than two points between 1980 and 2008.[10] This followed the publication of research by Michael Shayer in 2007,

---

[6] Extracted from DCSF data and from research by Cambridge Assessment. The data is restricted to 17-18 year old candidates in England taking 3 or more A levels and includes General Studies and Critical Thinking.

[7] Louise Armstead, "Sir Stuart Rose: Schools are not providing workers with the right skills", http://www.telegraph.co.uk/education/educationnews/6638699/Sir-Stuart-Rose-Schools-are-not-providing-workers-with-the-right-skills.html (accessed November 24th 2009).

[8] Jennifer Creevy, "Sir Terry Leahy lambasts government over education", http://www.retail-week.com/careers/sir-terry-leahy-lambasts-government-over-education/5007119.article (accessed October 13th 2009).

[9] In interview with Jeff Randall, Sky News, October 14th 2009.

[10] Richard Gray, "British teenagers have lower IQs than their counterparts did 30 years ago", http://www.telegraph.co.uk/education/educationnews/4548943/British-teenagers-have-lower-IQs-than-their-counterparts-did-30-years-ago.html (accessed February 7th 2009). Report refers to James Flynn, "Requiem for nutrition as the cause of IQ gains: Raven's gains in Britain 1938–2008", Economics & Human Biology (2009) http://www.sciencedirect.com/science?_ob=ArticleURL&_udi=B73DX-4VHGC2H-1&_user=1495569&_coverDate=03%2F31%2F2009&_alid=1127156823&_rdoc=1&_fmt=high&_orig=search&_cdi=11482&_sort=r&_docanchor=&view=c&_ct=1&_acct=C000053194&_version=1&_urlVersion=0&_userid=1495569&md5=adb4ce65dbea4eda6b3237c894fd235c> (accessed February 2nd 2009).

which claimed that English children in Year 7 are now "on average between two and three years behind where they were 15 years ago".[11]

Such findings are controversial. In trying to understand them, Shayer and Flynn point to the effect of a visually orientated youth culture, the culture of the video game and the text message. Shayer also refers to the impact on deep learning of teaching to the test, one of the consequences of the widespread use of exam and test results for accountability. Irrespective of whether one accepts their analysis, it highlights some worrying trends, the origin of which is anchored in socio-political as well as educational developments.

In the context of A levels, an exam that started in 1951 as a selection test for admission to HE has had to adapt as the proportion of 18 year olds taking it has risen from 6.8 to 46.3%,[12] the result of a policy of promoting higher levels of participation in order to support the demands of a growing and more complex economy though, as Alison Wolf has pointed out, it does not follow that the "vast amounts of public spending on education have been the key determinant of how rich we are today".[13] A qualification designed for the top end of the ability range therefore has now to serve the needs of a much broader constituency.

Side by side with this there has been a diversification and expansion in the number of subjects examined. When A levels started there were only 32 subjects. With the introduction of a number of new and applied disciplines this had risen to 69 by the time of the introduction of Curriculum 2000.[14] In parallel, reflecting more general social developments and prompted in particular by the rapid growth of information technology, the focus of syllabuses moved from knowledge to skills.

This has been accompanied by a steady extension of state involvement in the design and detail of the curriculum. This started with the introduction of the National Curriculum following the 1988 Education Act. There had previously

---

[11] John Crace, "Children are less able than they used to be" http://www.guardian.co.uk/education/2006/jan/24/schools.uk (accessed January 24th 2006). Report refers to Michael Shayer, Denise Ginsburg and Robert Coe, "Thirty years on - a large anti-Flynn effect? The Piagetian test Volume & Heaviness norms 1975 - 2003", *British Journal of Educational Psychology*, 77: 1 (2007) http://bpsoc.publisher.ingenta connect.com/search/download?pub=infobike%3a%2f%2fbpsoc%2fbjep%2f2007%2f00 000077%2f00000001%2fart00002&mimetype=text%2fhtml (accessed March 24th 2007).
[12] Figures taken from Higginson Report 1988 and DfES data.
[13] Alison Wolf, *Does Education Matter?* (London, 2002), p.xii.
[14] A-level subjects 1951 derived from Examinations 16-18 DES (1980), and A-level subjects 2000 derived from the QCA Statistics Team (2001).

been a long period, culminating in the 1975 scandal of the William Tyndale School, during which high levels of local and school level autonomy had led to widespread fears about capture of the school system by educational progressives. This was the background to Jim Callaghan's 1976 Ruskin speech calling for a national debate about education. The prevailing climate was still so antipathetic to central government's taking an interest in education that Bernard Donoughue, Callaghan's policy director at No 10, recalled the Department of Education being "deeply shocked that a prime minister should have the impertinence to trespass into its own secret garden".[15]

Callaghan's speech started the process of opening up that secret garden. In the world of curriculum and assessment the subsequent centralisation led to the creation of the exams Quango, the Qualifications and Curriculum Authority (QCA) which, with its predecessor bodies, wrested ownership of exam standards from the Awarding Bodies and was responsible for the National Curriculum. This created a structural conflict of interest, which was in turn aggravated by the QCA's close relationship with the Department of Education and Skills (now DCSF).[16] The result was that the QCA gave primacy to the execution of policy initiatives such as Curriculum 2000 and Diplomas over and above its responsibility for the stewardship of standards. It also absorbed the culture of an institutionalised expectation of ever rising standards that has been such a feature of education policy over the last decade.

The realisation that the qualification system was, as a result, hopelessly compromised has driven the Government to attempt to distance itself from qualifications regulation through the establishment of a new independent regulator, Ofqual. The hope is that this will restore trust in the system, and put an end to the annual dumbing down debate.[17]

Will it work? It is unlikely so long as the Government continues to exercise control through ownership of the curriculum. Whilst there is a legitimate concern about accountability here, bureaucratic activism, the increasing use of the curriculum as a vehicle of social policy and the need to reconcile competing

---

[15] Bernard Donoughue, *The Heat of the Kitchen*, (London , 2004), p.281.

[16] A Memorandum of Understanding   http://www.qcda.gov.uk/4979.aspx   (accessed December 7th 2009), agreed following the A level crisis of 2002, sought to define a division of responsibility between the department and the regulator. However, enquiries into delivery failures by the QCA of National Curriculum Tests in 2004 and 2008 both highlighted high levels of continuing day to day involvement by the Department in the QCA's activities.

[17] See DCSF consultation document "Confidence in Standards" (March 10th 2008), which stated that the plans to create Ofqual will "ensure that standards of qualification and assessment are maintained and can command the full confidence of the public".

interests among stakeholders mean that no doubt well-intentioned efforts to ensure consistent minimum standards in practice lead to idiosyncratic and frequently altered programmes of study.

We can see this if we look at what has happened to the National Curriculum in science. Here, the curriculum reflects the tension between the desire to promote general scientific literacy among non-scientists and the need to educate the next generation of practising scientists. The consequence is that content has been changed many times and progressively reduced. The Statutory Content for Key Stage 3 Science, for example, no longer identifies as a necessary part of the programme of study key concepts such as photosynthesis and the conservation of mass but does seek to promote the importance of healthy eating and regular exercise.[18]

In an effort to be motivating and inclusive, the National Curriculum has, therefore, come to include coverage of all sorts of essentially extraneous social issues. In doing so it has ceased to provide the statement of a common core of learning that was its original purpose and that is a characteristic of curriculum materials in educationally high performing nations.[19]

Examples of the faddishness and incoherence this can lead to abound. In January 2008 Ed Balls, announcing a programme to introduce compulsory cooking lessons, appealed to the public for suggestions as to which recipes should be included in a guide for schools.[20] Still on the theme of food, the QCA felt impelled in September 2009 to advise secondary school teachers to do more to incorporate food and farming into their lessons, advice explained by the QCA's Director of Curriculum on the Delphic grounds that "the curriculum encourages rather than prescribes going out in to the countryside and in to farms".[21] On a different note, the Government announced in November 2009 that lessons in gender equality and preventing violence in relationships will be compulsory in the PSHE curriculum from 2011.[22]

---

[18] See http://curriculum.qcda.gov.uk/uploads/QCA-07-3344-p_Science_KS3_tcm8413. pdf?return=/key-stages-3-and-4/subjects/science/keystage3/index.aspx (accessed December 8th 2009).
[19] See William H Schmidt and Richard S Prawat, "Curriculum coherence and national control of education: issue or non-issue?", *Journal of Curriculum Studies*, Volume 38, Number 6th (2006), p.641.
[20] DCSF press release, January 22nd 2008.
[21] Sue Horner speaking on Farming Today, BBC Radio 4, October 2nd 2009.
[22] See "School lessons to tackle domestic violence outlined",
http://news.bbc.co.uk/1/hi/uk/8376943.stm (accessed November 25th 2009).

What this illustrates is the extent to which the National Curriculum has strayed from its original purpose and become at once both overblown and hollowed out. It is not the role of the National Curriculum to act as a vehicle for a constantly shifting menu of flavour-of-the-month social concerns. What we need instead is a map setting out key concepts and a framework for progression, not a manifesto. The consequence, ironically, is that the generalised statements of scientific activity and application the National Curriculum actually contains are open to all sorts of inappropriate variation in interpretation – thereby creating scope for precisely that variability in teaching and learning that the National Curriculum is designed to prevent.

We therefore have the paradox that the application of central control – in this instance through the instrument of the National Curriculum – destabilises the learning it is designed to protect, a good illustration of why approaches to curriculum ownership and development now need re-thinking.

The National Curriculum extends only to 16, but the long hand of central control continues thereafter in the form of highly prescriptive, Ofqual specified A level qualification and subject criteria. These reduce flexibility, restrict the scope for Awarding Bodies and other interested parties to innovate and inhibit the alignment of curriculum, teaching and assessment that is desirable to achieve the best educational results.

There have been calls recently, reacting to this, for HE institutions to become involved in the development of subject syllabuses for A levels.[23] This is an attractive idea as it would permit HE, Awarding Bodies and schools to re-connect and re-establish ownership of the curriculum, instead of its being mediated as at present through regulatory and other central points of control. Awarding Bodies would welcome such a development and would be able to respond quickly and effectively, not least as this would be more likely than any regulatory reform to protect standards and deliver long term confidence in the public exam system.

We should therefore have an urgent debate about how to move this forward. To be effective, there would need to be recurrent funding streams and appropriate career recognition for participating academics. HE engagement would in addition need to be coherently structured and involve the sector as a whole, not just individual institutions.

We also need as part of the same process to move towards a less ambitious National Curriculum. This should set out a core framework, beyond which teaching professionals, Awarding Bodies, representatives of HE and other

---

[23] See, for example, Reform report "Core Business" (2009).

interested bodies can create interesting and challenging learning programmes on the ground; programmes, in other words, which incorporate a slimmed down National Curriculum but go well beyond it.

This would need to be a long term strategy. If successful, however, a future Secretary of State, echoing Ken Clarke, would again be able to assert that these matters were largely beyond their control; they would do so this time with satisfaction rather than regret, and in the knowledge that their lack of control was a powerful force for that liberation of learning that this book is all about.

EDUCATION FOR 21ST CENTURY BUSINESS

Stuart Rose and John May

"Great Britain is falling behind its European competitors because of the failure of its education system to keep pace with the extent of change in industry."

It reads like a headline from a recent edition of the Today programme, but it is actually an extract from the 1884 Samuelson Committee's report on the state of Britain's technical education.

Ever since then, and quite possibly before, generations of interested parties have debated the role of education in preparing young people for the world of work: what sorts of skills, behaviours and attitudes do employers need to see in the next generation? What should business itself be doing to make a difference?

The debate continues. For the last twenty-five years, Business in the Community, HRH the Prince of Wales's organisation dedicated to campaigning for responsible business, has championed forging closer links between the worlds of commerce and education.

Successive governments have set up task forces, committees and commissions to examine what young people should know about the world of work and just how they might learn it. A whole industry has grown up to broker partnerships between business and education.

And yet many schools continue to mistrust the motives of businesses who offer to support pupils' learning. Many employers continue to complain about the work readiness of their newest recruits, and countless young people struggle to work out what they want to do in life.

Three challenges face us in delivering a credible system of education – credible for employers and for students and their families:

- Tackling our long-held cultural scepticism about vocational education.

- Coming to accept that the world for which we are preparing young people looks nothing like the world we knew even five years ago.
- Beginning to explore the possibility that schools and education may need to undergo a massive revolution.

The challenges are, of course, interlinked.

Can the British ever value a vocational education as highly as a purely academic one? It isn't as if we haven't tried to put job-related courses into the mainstream of secondary schools before. We know that we need to engage and motivate pupils who don't find academic programmes relevant. We also know that there's a growing deficit in employment skills. Business in the Community has estimated that within ten years, the UK could have a shortfall of nearly 50% in its skilled taskforce across craft, technical and practical skills. This is a shaming statistic in a country boasting generations of compulsory education, and one which poses some demanding challenges for us all.

There has been a recent move to create a new qualification to blur the edges between academic and vocational study. This has been presented as the third of three equally meritorious routes: academic (GCSE, A-level, university) work based (apprenticeships) and a middle way, the Diploma, preparation either for employment or for entry to higher education.

This is not an entirely new approach. There have been work-based programmes in schools for many years, including those offered by the vocational award bodies, RSA, City & Guilds and BTEC, such as Foundation Programmes and CPVE.

Given the time lag for any qualification to become recognised and respected, it is hard to see that the Diploma has really been given much of a chance. There is already talk of scrapping it, or at the very least organising a massive overhaul.

The fault lies not with the qualification itself, but with the way in which it is viewed by society. We have to change our attitude towards any qualification pathway that is not the "gold standard" A-level. We have to avoid treating it as a ghetto for the least able or as an educational or career cul-de-sac.

The world of work is changing. Our parents were prepared for careers that involved, for most of them, one job for life. Our generation tends to stick to one industry sector throughout its career, even if we change specific jobs several times. We cannot predict what the pattern for young people now in school will be, though it seems likely that they may move roles even more often than we do, interact globally and undertake jobs that have not yet even been invented.

The linked revolutions of developing technology, globalisation of markets, changing demographics and shifting personal values all contribute to ensuring that the adult world of today's school children will be very different from our own.

One thing we can say without any difficulty is that we are already living in a time of profound change – and the speed and extent of this change is going to intensify. We live in exponential times. The rate of technological change is seismic. We need to create flexible, resilient learners with the skills to enable them to cope well in a fast changing world.

If we are going to change our attitudes to education, if we're going to cope with the revolutions of change that are affecting our world, then we believe that we have re-engineer our education system.

We have got to stop seeing schools as separate entities and the teaching profession as a closed vocation. If you took a 19th Century doctor into a modern hospital they would be amazed at how things have changed in 100 years. We have had the discovery of penicillin, of DNA, of anti-virals.

If you took a 19th-Century teacher into most schools, they would see a scene not dissimilar from that which they themselves experienced. Serried ranks of young people being tutored by an individual, imparting knowledge.

We are fast entering a state of crisis in getting enough people to teach those young people. If we continue to run schools as we do currently, there could be an enormous shortfall by 2016.

We need a more flexible use of people supporting young people's learning, drawn from beyond school boundaries. There are examples of this happening already, but they are examples we haven not yet capitalised upon or built to scale.

Travel to West London and to British Airways' teaching centre in the grounds of their head offices. There you'll find employees, usually, but not exclusively, cabin crew, working with language students in aircraft mock ups, getting the students to use their modern foreign languages in real work situations.

Or visit the schools supported by the charity Young Enterprise and see business volunteers going into schools weekly, offering students direct experience of enterprise through working together to run their own real company.

Or go to the companies like M&S that are now beginning to host sixth form students through programmes like those run by Career Academies UK, providing young people with real projects that develop their understanding of business, and give them the chance to practise their employability skills and raise their aspirations.

Or, actually, go to any Education Business Partnership in the country – and its manager will show you similar examples of innovation and learning.

What they cannot show you yet, despite the work of several task forces and business-led campaigns, is a truly systematic approach by government to supporting such work, or a genuine proven commitment to providing resources to enable this good practice to build and spread.

We know that business benefits enormously from getting involved in education. The benefits include:

- Staff development and learning.
- The chance to innovate in a safe environment.
- The opportunity to bring energy, enthusiasm and openness into the company.
- The opportunities that exist to support staff recruitment and retention.
- Gaining and retaining new customers.
- The chance to improve the firm's image in the community.

But, whilst the rationale is sound, is there really enough interest or commitment – from schools and business – to build such partnerships to real scale?

Our vision of the 21ˢᵗ-Century school is one where businesses have an essential role to play in providing part time support for various parts of the curriculum, often working with small groups of students rather than whole tutor groups.

It is one where many of the students receive support from mentors, often via email as well as at 1:1 meetings. Teaching staff spend time on placements within companies, skilling themselves up in preparation for extended stays in industry and commerce or ensuring that their own teaching is up to date.

It is a vision where volunteers' enthusiasm, knowledge and real-life experiences enrich students' learning, helping them to understand the world of work, raise aspirations and prepare for their future. It is one where, at the same time, the volunteers also share in the learning experience, exploring and developing their own skills and knowledge alongside the students.

It is also one where all young people learn the basics about how business works, so that they can interact with commerce, as consumers, employees or employers when they are adults. Where all young people have the opportunity to develop the skills, behaviours and attitudes needed to take a constructive place in society, recognising that, for the vast majority, that means being prepared for the world of work. Where all young people get excellent advice, information and guidance, so that they can make effective decisions about the pathways they want to follow as they embark on their quite possibly unpredictable careers.

What will need to have happened to achieve this vision? The government and the private sector will both have committed long term resources to recognising the power of business and will have funded an effective brokering service for schools and companies who want to work together.

The very spirit of education is to make things happen – the challenge is to ride the waves of change and not to be overwhelmed by them.

THE PERSPECTIVES MODEL FOR THE EPQ

Elizabeth Swinbank and John Taylor

Perspectives on Science (PoS) is a course in History, Philosophy and Ethics of Science. Originally developed as an AS course, it is now a "designed programme" for the Edexcel Extended Project Qualification and is an archetype for the EPQ. We will first outline the PoS project then describe how the same model is being used in other areas of study.

Perspectives on Science

At an early stage of developing PoS, our awarding body proposed – initially as a cost-saving measure – that, rather than having an exam, the course should be assessed entirely through an individual student project marked by teachers and moderated by the awarding body. This was tremendously liberating. Rather than having to specify content that would be tested through mechanical recall, we devised an assessment scheme that focused firmly on skills of research, analysis, argumentation and presentation within the context of history, philosophy and ethics of science.

The PoS specification required that students should undertake a research project leading to a dissertation in a broadly defined scientific area. The project should involve literature research, with some consideration of the nature and reliability of sources, and should address a question that had a historical, ethical and/or philosophical dimension. The dissertation should be structured as an academic paper (abstract, introduction, literature review, discussion, conclusion, bibliography) and the main outcomes should also be communicated in a short oral presentation. Far from being restrictive, this structure helps students to organise and focus their work.

A key feature of a PoS project is that students should develop their own point of view on a research question, and that they should present a reasoned case for that point of view drawing on relevant literature and using appropriate vocabulary; for example, they might be expected to refer to ethical frameworks such as utilitarianism or divine command theory.

In order to undertake a PoS project successfully, students need a grounding in basic elements of history, philosophy and ethics of science. They also need to be able to carry out literature research, present arguments, and so on. These skills are not innate. We therefore developed a model for PoS in which individual project work is preceded by a taught course and supported by published course materials. Through a series of case studies drawing on a variety of scientific areas and based in different periods of history, students develop the knowledge and skills that will support their project work. They also encounter questions and issues that could be explored further in a project.

Having acquired some skills and developed their own thinking, PoS students then work on their projects under the supervision of a teacher. The teacher's role is crucial throughout the project work. Students need guidance first of all in devising an appropriate research proposal that is clearly focused and lends itself to some literature research and original thinking. Teachers then monitor and encourage progress through class seminars and reporting-back sessions and through one-to-one discussion. This teacher support, together with the structured nature of the PoS dissertation, helps ensure that students make steady progress towards well-defined milestones (such as drafting a literature review at an early stage of the project) and do not become daunted by the magnitude of the task.

With any coursework assessment, the issue of plagiarism must be considered. In PoS, this is addressed head-on by including lessons on plagiarism in the taught course. Students are taught what plagiarism is, why it is wrong, and how to avoid it; they are taught how to quote and reference source material correctly. While students are working on their projects, frequent contact with the teacher means that plagiarism is unlikely to go unnoticed. Finally, if students present their work orally to an audience, and answer questions on it, they will only be able to do this effectively if the work they describe is genuinely their own.

The experience of PoS in many centres has been both liberating and broadening. PoS projects have tackled a wide range of challenging questions, as diverse as "Should the UK abortion law be changed?", "Did anything exist before the Big Bang?", "How did the Copernican paradigm shift affect subsequent developments in cosmology?" and "Are wind turbines a good solution to the energy crisis?". When students are given the opportunity to explore a question arising from their own interests and concerns, they often put in a huge amount of effort and produce work of an impressively high standard.

In several centres, teachers from science and humanities departments have collaborated on the taught course and on the supervision of project work, and both they and their students have benefited from this broadening of their experience. Teachers are stimulated by the challenge of undertaking, with their students, genuine intellectual enquiry rather than "delivering" a prescribed specification. PoS students who are taking science subjects gain a wider perspective on their specialisms, those who are studying no other science post-16 are able to explore scientific issues in depth, and all PoS students benefit from the project work. Teachers and students alike recognise that the experience of independent working, and the skills students develop, provide an excellent foundation for both higher education and employment.

Extending Perspectives

Throughout the development of PoS, we were in discussion with the then QCA (now QCDA), who were very supportive of our work. When the new Diploma qualifications were announced, it was no surprise that student project work was a compulsory element.

A Diploma at Level 3 (equivalent to GCE) requires an Extended Project. The Extended Project Qualification (EPQ) is also available as a standalone qualification equivalent to 0.5 A-level in terms of UCAS points and funding (in the maintained sector) and requiring a similar number of guided learning hours. (Diplomas at Levels 1 and 2 (GCSE equivalent) also require learners to undertake a Project, albeit less ambitious than the EP. As a standalone qualification, a Level 1 or 2 Project is equivalent to 0.5 GCSE.). EPQs are offered by all three of the English awarding bodies, and PoS is assessed as an EPQ awarded by Edexcel. Currently the majority of centres offering the EPQ offer it as a standalone qualification.

The new project qualifications present a wealth of possibilities for project work. Some students research a question leading to a dissertation (as in PoS), while others undertake a laboratory or fieldwork investigation, or explore issues through a performance, or by designing and making an artefact. There is also scope for group work (particularly in performance-based projects), though individual contributions must be clearly identified.

Experience with PoS led us to develop what has become known as the Perspectives model for project work, which is applicable to all varieties of project, not just those leading to a dissertation. The PoS experience has helped us to characterise what is meant by an EP and distinguish the EP from a piece of subject-based coursework: an EP should be "extended" in the three dimensions of deepening understanding, broadening skills and widening perspectives. That is, students should explore an issue in depth, develop some new skills, and look beyond a single subject or discipline.

One key feature of a Perspectives EP is that students research some information and evaluate their sources. All projects will require some secondary research, and some might also involve primary research where students collect their own data from laboratory or fieldwork or using questionnaire surveys.

Another key feature is that students acquire and demonstrate some critical thinking skills. That is, they should develop their own ideas about their project work, and be able to present and defend those ideas. One fruitful way of approaching this is for students to explore an ethical or philosophical issue relating to their project area.

A third key feature is that there should be a structured report of the project. In some cases, this is a substantial dissertation which is the sole final outcome of the project work, while in others it is a relatively short report accompanying another outcome such as an artefact or a performance. While the precise structure is not prescribed, we strongly recommend that reports are presented under distinct headings (abstract, research review, discussion/development/ analysis, conclusion/evaluation, bibliography), as this helps students to focus their work and break the project down into manageable tasks.

Perspectives EPs also share the generic features of all projects: students must plan, organise and record their work. But while these aspects are important, and students do need to organise and document their work, they are not the be all and end all of doing a project. In a Perspectives-type project, there should not be an excessive focus on form-filling, logging and box-ticking. Rather, the emphasis should be firmly on researching, thinking and doing.

Anyone who has ever carried out a project of any sort will know that a key to success is to start from the right place. So a final (or perhaps that should be "initial") key feature of a Perspectives-type project is the proposal. Students need to identify an area that interests them and then to develop a question or brief for their project. The most successful projects tend to be those with a well-focused question that lends itself to some literature research and some original work as outlined above. But writing a good project proposal is not easy, and students need both preparation and guidance.

An overarching feature of the Perspectives model is that project work is preceded by a taught course where students develop their skills and explore some issues relating to the general area of their project. Then, as in PoS, students are in a good position to write a project proposal and plan and carry out their work.

To support the taught course for the EP, we have developed a "Lego kit" of resources and suggested lesson plans. The intention is that teachers use these materials, maybe along with others of their own devising, to construct their own taught course for their own students. Some of the materials are generic to all projects (eg students learn how to research information, evaluate sources, plan their time, analyse arguments, communicate their ideas), while some are specific to certain types of project outcome (eg writing a questionnaire, developing a design brief, planning a rehearsal schedule, carrying out fieldwork). Other materials present case studies relating to a wide range of study areas (eg business, expressive arts, technology, professional values). Here, students engage in research and discussion activities to develop their skills, and meet a variety of issues that have the potential for further development and exploration in project work. The study areas are quite broad, allowing teachers to select materials that relate to particular GCE subjects or to Diploma lines of learning.

Finally and not least, teachers have a key role in the Perspectives model. While students should of course be using their own ideas, planning their time and working fairly independently, teachers need to supervise their work. Class seminars, reporting-back sessions and one-to-one discussions all help to keep students on track and guard against plagiarism.

We believe that all these elements (taught course, on-going teacher supervision, background research, critical thinking skills, focused project proposal, structured report) are highly desirable, if not essential, for good project work. Without these, it is all too easy for students to spend a lot of time on a project, but at the same time gain very little in terms of transferable knowledge and skills; the end product of such a project is often of poor quality and does not reflect the ability of the student or the effort that they put into their work.

Students from a wide variety of backgrounds and with a broad range of interests have responded well to the Perspectives approach and we have already seen some impressive EPs. Projects can be as diverse as the students undertaking them, and range over such topics as cyber bullying (which might be explored through performance), ethical issues about open-source software, questions about business practice (such as whether Google should trade in China) and plans for a kinetic sculpture of DNA for the atrium of a school science department. As with the original PoS development, it seems that the EPQ has genuine potential for fostering high quality work from a great many students.

EPQ

Sarah Fletcher

The Extended Project Qualification (EPQ) is perhaps the most liberating educational innovation of recent years. To see quite how exciting it is, we need first to look at the context.

Education in England since the beginning of this century has manoeuvred itself, quite unintentionally, into something of a cul-de-sac. Modular examinations in 2000 were hailed by many as the great democratizer, allowing students more than one opportunity to get it right without the sudden death of the old A levels. Academic examinations were thereby brought more into line with the traditional vocational approach to education. The rationalisation of the old plethora of Examination Boards, which ran alongside this reform, paved the way for more consistent expectations and firmer ground on which to build recognised standards. Education in England was brought up to date and doors were opened for those who had previously seen the sixth form and university as elitist and unattractive. The ideals were right and detractors of the current system sometimes lose sight of the failings of the past. As is often the case, however, the implementation of change can bring unintended consequences and the educational reforms of the early 21st century were no exception.

The ability to take and retake material until the marks are right is disruptive of progress and takes time and focus away from the development of skills and understanding for the next stage. Chopping syllabuses into four or six separate units has resulted in a fragmented approach to learning, while uniform mark schemes tend to place ease of assessment over creativity and have encouraged a formulaic approach to examination success. The result has been growing criticism: subject knowledge has been allegedly "dumbed down" in order to make A levels more accessible; grade inflation has inevitably followed in the wake of retake opportunities; students are too reliant on teacher direction as analysing mark schemes has become an end in itself; study skills have lost out under pressure of time and the ability to work independently seems to have disappeared along the way. We love measuring success with solid, well understood qualifications but the current methods of assessment are now losing credibility. Since when was education ever easy? The tension between making examinations accessible to a wide audience and stretching the top end has always existed and there is no simple solution. Neither is there an easy answer to the future. Education is under challenge as rapid technological change makes second guessing the world of tomorrow extraordinarily difficult. We now speak of the need for transferable skills; a flexible approach to life and to work rather than predetermined training but the school curriculum has yet to match expectation with practice. A new approach is needed, which redefines what we really mean by education.

The Extended Project Qualification may just be the opportunity we need. While retaining many of the ideals and benefits of the new system it succeeds in overriding the disadvantages. At level 3 it counts as half an A-level and it provides a vehicle for promoting independent learning skills in research, analysis, argument and presentation. Although there has to be some sort of written report, nonetheless students can express their ideas in more creative forms through an artefact, or a performance, for example, making it accessible and engaging. The EPQ is optional at A-level but it is embedded in all the new Diplomas. It therefore bridges the gap between academic study and vocational approaches to education, leaving the door open to all sorts of ideas and interpretations. The EPQ sits very well, therefore, within the ideal of widening opportunities and of encouraging participation. The experience of those who teach it shows that it provides just the stimulus for progression which we need. Self motivation, study skills and creativity lie at its heart as projects are researched and presented often to higher standards than one would normally expect at school level. Educationalists speak of the need for deep learning and higher order thinking skills to be based on intrinsic rather than on extrinsic imperatives and here we have the perfect opportunity to allow students to prove their worth by exploring their own ideas and interests. Research projects can be on topics of personal choice, they can help to further a desire to engage in more abstract or creative avenues or to they can relate to a particular university or career aspiration. Although based on freedom of choice, the EPQ is assessed within a recognised framework and is a nationally accepted qualification, thereby preserving our desire for all things to be measurable. It is both relevant and accessible to a wide range of abilities and, given the right preconditions, it opens the way for levels of attainment which humble expectations. From a student's point of view, the EPQ can be truly liberating.

In describing our experience at Rugby, I would like to suggest other ways in which the EPQ can act as an important catalyst for change.

From the beginning we recognised that core skills need developing before students are let loose on personal research. To argue a case convincingly, having met with different perspectives and contradictory points of view in the research phase, is not always easy, while sorting and selecting evidence and presenting ideas clearly and cogently are high order skills. John Taylor's chapter on Perspectives on Science sets the scene. Our approach at Rugby similarly focuses on providing students with an opportunity to engage in ethical and philosophical debate alongside training in critical thinking and clear advice on research and presentation. Ethics and philosophy may have been born in the Classical World but it is interesting how relevant they are in education today. They provide an important framework for analysing problems and for developing skills in argument and debate. Creativity is born of challenging ideas and of questioning preconceived notions and these are the sorts of attributes our educational system should be promoting. John and his team produced a wonderful vehicle for discussing scientific themes and we were determined to diversify the methodology.

Staff at Rugby were given the opportunity to discuss possible cross curricular courses which could sit alongside Perspectives on Science and which could stimulate interest and ideas for research amongst students in a variety of different contexts. This was not to be an opportunity for the delivery of more content but a vehicle for generating discussion in areas of general interest and for breaking down subject barriers. The result is a wonderful array of preparatory courses which are designed to develop thinking skills and to be thought provoking. They enable students to engage in some of the great debates of the modern world and in doing so they force them to clarify their own thinking and to understand alternative points of view. "Culture and Identity", for example, blends English with History and the Classical World while "People Power and Wealth" brings together Business, Economics and Politics. We have courses for those interested in Performance, Engineering, Digital Innovation and Global Issues. These courses have arisen though student interest and staff expertise and are wonderfully creative in bringing departments together in developing relevant material and in discussing approaches to learning. Used imaginatively, this is a very powerful educational tool. It builds on the notion of personal choice, while capturing the imagination of teaching staff who can engage in the business of teaching and learning in an examination free environment.

The whole experiment raises important questions about education in general. Allowing students more control over their own learning, giving them space to make mistakes and to work things out for themselves, can be far more productive in the long run than more traditional approaches. It is designed to produce the robust and interesting individuals that universities and employers are asking for.

I described the school devised courses as an offshoot of individual choice, an attempt to make sure that students remain engaged and interested and that they are given the right frameworks on which to hang their own ideas and research. There is a related possibility which is equally exciting. Universities and employers are usually divorced from the construction of school syllabuses and from the methods of assessment we use. The opportunity of working collaboratively with local bodies in putting together relevant introductory courses as described above has huge potential and the EPQ opens the door for this to happen. Joint ventures which begin to tie educational and employment more closely together and which allow students to explore the themes and concerns of the world beyond school could give individual ideas a real context within which to work. We have already begun the process through university contacts for "Culture and Identity". "Engineering" and "Digital Innovation" are also under discussion. The possibilities are exciting and potentially transformational. As one university professor put it, why leave this to the Sixth Form? Shouldn't we be beginning much earlier in the primary schools? Everything is possible with a little imagination and a willingness to work together. The door is open and we need the vision to push it as wide as possible.

The main focus of this essay has been the Sixth Form. Equally interesting are the possibilities for the EPQ lower down the school with the Qualification now on offer at levels 1 and 2. At Rugby we use the Level 2 Project as a vehicle for discussing themes on Citizenship, encouraging group research and class debate on issues such as democracy, the role of Government and environmental challenges. The same focus on independent study, ethics and philosophy pervades, building skills for the future. Growing confidence in independent learning throughout the School is designed to impact on every subject and to raise standards through a more critical and exploratory approach to learning. It was one of my privileges to watch the final presentations made by a group of NEETS in Warwickshire in a project devised by the Education Development Service (EDS). These young people had chosen to produce a video about their experiences and to rewrite all the literature relating to those in similar situations for the Warwickshire website. The research they engaged in for both the video and the website was wide ranging and impressive and the final results were extraordinarily good. These people had dropped out of education and had no qualifications to their name. Although not formally an EPQ, one could see, nonetheless, how this sort of approach to learning could engage interest where a more standard delivery of the school curriculum would simply fail to hit the mark. At all levels, the EPQ is a powerful educational tool and one with considerable potential.

Described like this, the EPQ becomes something of a Trojan horse, driving change from within the curriculum. It is my hope that the liberating model of learning the EPQ exemplifies will take root and that we will learn to trust it and to build on it as we develop a truly modern approach to education.

RAISING ASPIRATIONS BY MENTORING

Nigel Bowles

Raising Aspirations and Widening Participation is a theme with special resonance and importance for research universities. The University of Oxford shares the obligation among those universities to attract those with the greatest potential to do outstanding intellectual work. The imperative is general across the University: in the recruitment of research and teaching staff, of graduate students, and of undergraduates. Far from being a politically fashionable political commitment recently acquired, Oxford's commitment rather lies as it has long lain – at the centre of its values as one of the world's leading research and teaching institutions.

As is the case at other universities, academics at Oxford focus upon its outreach projects including those under the *Aim Higher* rubric with the aim of raising aspirations and widening participation. They work with the Sutton Trust and other organizations with purposes congruent with Oxford's own; have good working relations with hundreds of state schools across the UK; and invest much energy and imagination in encouraging undergraduate applications from populations with little history of participation in higher education. The cultural obstacles are often great, but the results achieved as a result of the partnership with school teachers and their students are promising.

Through its own Admissions Information Centre; multiple visits to schools across the UK; its extensive and energetic participation in Higher Education Fairs and in the Further Education Access Initiative; University, Departmental, and College Open Days; Oxford and Cambridge Regional Conferences; its active support for the Target Schools programme; in Year 12 Science Master-classes; Chemistry Connect, and Physics Outreach; Marcus' Marvellous Mathemagicians; and the Women in Science Spring Residential Programme, Oxford already has a suite of programmes and activities designed to raise aspirations and widen participation. The work of Oxford's *Black Boys Can* programme is but one of several targeted initiatives that Oxford's Admissions Director and his colleagues have led. With support from Oxford's own many ethnic minority students, this programme and others make a difference not just to the University's undergraduate profile, but to the lives of those hundreds of school students whom they reach, encourage, and support.

Much the same is true of each of the colleges' own Open Days, outreach projects, and mentoring programmes. Individual Fellows, Lecturers, and Admissions Tutors in every undergraduate college in the University also strive to attract those with the intellectual potential to benefit from the intensive and interactive education offered at Oxford, and to find that potential in school (and mature) students from wherever they may come and whatever their circumstances. What is true of Oxford is, of course, true of many other Universities across the UK in the Russell Group, Mainstream, and post-'92 institutions. Available data, supplemented by personal conversations, show me that those many colleagues at Oxford with responsibilities for undergraduate admissions devote much time and energy in trying to find ways to improve participation rates. My colleagues' objects in this respect are aligned not just with the University's own interest but with what those colleagues rightly understand to be a clear public interest: to attract the best-qualified students with the greatest potential for intellectual creativity – the most powerful form of public good.

Yet despite the high quality of such outreach activity and the clarity of view about research universities' purposes, participation rates by members not only of lower-decile socio-economic groups but of middle decile groups in those universities remains much lower either than university academics wish or than society ought to tolerate. Mitigating the problem is entirely achievable by an appropriately-scaled and designed mentoring programme in the UK, drawing upon existing pools of expertise, experience, and enthusiasm in universities to have decisive, and decisively beneficial, effects upon the aspiration and participation of young people in higher education. Much mentoring already exists in UK universities, as it does (not least in e-form) at Oxford.[1] Yet excellent though most of the work in the UK is, fragmentation blunts its effect. A mentoring programme, imaginatively designed to an appropriate scale, would complement and energise not just Oxford's own project to stimulate intellectual interest and ambition among young people, but parallel projects of other UK universities in the Russell, Mainstream, and post -'92 groups.

Oxford's outreach is most effective when those colleagues and students give off the electricity that they feel in conveying the value and rewards of stretching abilities, raising intellectual aspirations, and building mentees' confidence to meet intellectual challenges. Such stretching of abilities, raising of aspirations, and building of confidence are the very things that those same colleagues already do

---

[1] See://www.ox.ac.uk/admissions/undergraduate_courses/working_with_schools_ and_colleges/ementoring.html (last accessed 12th February 2010).

for each other in their daily professional lives within the academy as they engage in research with their graduate students and in teaching with their undergraduates. Academics in all universities are thereby already daily engaged in lifting aspirations. Because Oxford by no means caters primarily to the brilliant finished product of popular fable, academics here already do just that more frequently than some without such teaching experience might suppose. Since these are our teaching and learning skills within this University, it would seem right to project them and their supporting culture of evangelising enthusiasm into the schools where there is latent talent and ability ready to respond to appropriate encouragement and motivation.

Mentoring which draws upon existing expertise and enthusiasm works. We know that it does so because experience in Israel and New Zealand (by means of an adapted policy transfer) confirms it. As Vice-Chancellor of the University of Auckland before he took up the post of Vice-Chancellor at Oxford, Dr John Hood sought to identify the best outreach programme in the world from which he and his colleagues might learn and then adapt both to Auckland's needs and strengths and to New Zealand's social circumstances whilst ensuring scalability. He found it in the *Perach* programme in Israel whose Director, Amos Carmeli, he asked to assist him and his colleagues in designing the framework for Auckland's own mentoring programme.[2]

That is how *MATES* (Mentoring and Tutoring Education Scheme), inspired by Israeli experience, originated and came to be implemented in 2002. *MATES* works with those year 12-13 students whom their schools identify as 'having the potential to succeed in tertiary education'. Through a combination of mentoring and tutoring, *MATES* seeks, in the University of Auckland's own words, "... to encourage academic achievement, raise aspirations and enhance self-confidence". It does so by linking successful University students with matched secondary school students. The individual mentoring relationship is the key to success but is supplemented both by tutoring of school students in small groups and small seminars focussed upon building organizational skills.

The University of Auckland set three objectives for the *MATES* programme:

1. That all involved in the programme (mentees; their families; school teachers) involved in the programme should find their experience of *MATES* positive and worthwhile;

---

[2] For details, see http://www.perach.org.il/Perach/Templates/ShowPage.asp? DBID=1&LNGID=2&TMID=10000&FID=317.

2.   that the mentees and school teachers report improved confidence, aspirations and achievement by each mentee; and

3.   that the university mentors report at the end of the year an enhanced awareness of social problems, and that they have found the experience developmentally worthwhile.

The programme succeeded. Good results were apparent even at a decile one school, helping to generate ten admissions to Bachelor degree programmes. Two of the programme's mentees from decile one to three schools won scholarships to enable them to study at the University of Auckland in 2006. 84.2% of *MATES* students in year 12 in 2004 achieved national level 2 certificate compared with the national average of 43% for students from decile 1-3 schools; all of the year 12 students mentored in 2004 returned to study in 2005 to complete their secondary schooling; 82% of the year 13 students in 2004 from a decile 1-3 school progressed to post-secondary education in 2005 compared with only 31% in 1999; 53% of the year 13 students in 2004 from a decile 1-3 school enrolled at universities in 2005 compared with 1999 statistics of 12%; and in 2005, approximately three quarters of Year 13 *MATES* participants proceeded to enrol at New Zealand universities.

MATES is a much smaller scheme than *Perach* which operates nationally. Scalable, organizationally robust, *Perach* has a record of achievement which would be impressive under any circumstances but is especially so given the fractured condition of Israeli society. *Perach* confronts social fractures head on by setting itself an ambitious objective:

"To develop and enrich Jewish and Arab children from disadvantaged families through a close relationship with a person acting as both tutor and mentor, and thereby to reduce social and educational differences among children."

Organized as a national and apolitical project with a simple management structure, *Perach* requires that those selected to act as mentors simply be "... good and motivated people" whose first concern is with their mentees' needs. Recruiting tutors annually, usually in the late summer and early autumn, *Perach* requires them to commit to participate in the project for at least one academic year.

The Minister of Education appoints members of *Perach*'s public board which in turn elects a management group from among its members. The structure is pyramidal, with a small head office located at the Weizmann Institute of Science; regional branches; and offices located in universities. Managers of each regional branch supervise between 50 and 70 coordinators, all of whom are students (and themselves former mentors), and each of whom manages between 45 and 50 mentors. Coordinators identify appropriate pairings of mentors and mentees, and thereafter counsel mentors individually and, where appropriate, convene plenary discussion groups to identify improvements to mentoring practice. Universities coordinate with the Education Ministry, local authorities, and school managers in actively supporting *Perach* Ministry. *Perach*'s revenue streams from the Council for Higher Education; two government departments; universities and colleges; and local governments is supplemented by funding provided by benefactors. In 2009, approximately 58,000 children in 1,300 schools benefited from Perach programmes, supported by 30,000 mentors.

One of the special projects in which *Perach* has invested its expertise and energy has particular significance for the UK – that of educating, inspiring, and enthusing disadvantaged immigrants. *Tutorship for Immigrants* is an innovative tutorship project in partnership with *Perach* and Ono Academic College to assist children of new immigrants in their studies and adjustment to the educational and social system.[3] The purpose behind it is to create a cycle of giving in which new immigrant students receive academic assistance from established students through *Perach* (whose scholarships it finances) in addition to scholarships for tuition in return for tutoring children of new immigrants from their ethnic group. A virtuous chain of giving is thereby created, to public and private benefit.

Four key lessons may be drawn from *Perach* and *MATES*. All find confirmation in the achievements of regional and local mentoring schemes in the UK across the ability range:

> *firstly*, mentors can and do enthuse young people about learning at school;

> *secondly*, with such enthusiasm, young people can and do commit to their learning;

> *thirdly*, they thereby lift their self-esteem; and

> *fourthly*, they consequently stretch themselves and measurably raise their levels of achievement.

The quantified results are plain: *Perach* and *MATES* mentoring schemes have improved and enriched the lives of mentors, mentees, school teachers, and supplying universities. In the latter connection, there is no more reliable source

---

[3] See http://www.ono.ac.il/?CategoryID=336.

than Colin Prentice who, on his retirement as Schools Director at the University of Auckland, observed that:

> "After a lifetime in education, including wonderful years as Principal of two secondary schools, I would consider MATES one of the highlights of my life. It is one of the best educational programmes I have ever been involved with. The results are just staggering, with university enrolments from the MATES schools at about three times the average for decile one to three schools."

We in the UK need to catch and stretch promising students early enough, encouraging them to think about academic subjects in academic ways. To do so requires the building of confidence through reading and independent thinking about what is read; creative, critical, and analytical independence in problem-solving; the development of clear oral and written communication, and even moral courage. These are all things that employers want; they are decisively qualities that a civilized and literate nation requires. A national mentoring project can be designed to foster them all, and thereby support and strengthen student-centred liberal education. No research university should presume to tell schools how to do their jobs. But what research universities can do is to show school students both that the education that they can get at such universities is profoundly liberating, and that through mentoring the intensity of university education can energise and enthuse school students and, in the literal sense, educate them by drawing out their potential.

Evidence shows the importance of raising the aspirations of school children as a means of widening participation in universities in general, and in research universities in particular. Regional mentoring initiatives with similar objectives, such as that run successfully by Cardiff University, have enjoyed much success. So, too, have programmes such as Teach First, and a number of programmes managed by individual universities, and by departments and student organizations within universities, and by Oxford and Cambridge colleges. These initiatives nevertheless share a problem of fragmentation in which much fine work is being done less efficiently and effectively than it would if brought under the umbrella of a national mentoring organization. The Israeli and New Zealand cases suggest that in designing policy to achieve the intermediate objective of raising aspirations and the fundamental objective of widening participation, the programme should be national in scope and vision, and enjoy complete support nationally from government, universities, schools, and professional bodies.

I write for myself, not on behalf of an institution. But I am confident that, with government support both full and sincere, UK academics would contribute energetically to a national mentoring programme. Alas, attempts to engage successive UK ministers in serious discussion about a national mentoring policy have met with less interest or optimism than the evidence of success elsewhere warrants. The UK Government has supported two mentoring schemes since 1999: the National Mentoring Pilot Project (NMPP) (1999–2004), and the National Mentoring Scheme (NMS) (2004–2006). Both were successful. The NMPP and NMS schemes provided support to school students (13–19 year olds) from deprived areas through a system of mentoring in which trained, supported and remunerated university students visited identified pupils (mentees) in local schools and worked with them regularly on a one-to-one basis. The mentors supported the mentees' individual learning and development needs, and thereby helped them to address deficiencies of self-worth, persistence, confidence, aspirations, goal setting and time management.

In an independent evaluation of the NMPP (2005), academic researchers at Warwick University found that mentoring schemes of one year's duration that were strongly supported by the head and the teaching staff of schools had the effect of raising pupils' achievement by one to two grades in GCSE in English, maths and science compared to their control group. Similarly, at Key Stage 3, mentoring for a year in supportive schools raised achievement by between half a level and one level in the three core subjects.

Given the scale and density of socially-concentrated educational failure in the UK, the weakness of educational culture in many demographic groups, and the pervasiveness of low expectations in many of those groups, the need for action on grounds both of moral urgency and economic utility is overwhelming. There is no reason why a national mentoring system cannot now be established which draws upon the lessons learned in Israel, New Zealand, and in the UK's own NMPP and NMS to:

- raise the mentees' standards of performance and improve their GCSE, GCE/VCE, A and AS-level grades and achievement in such other vocational qualifications as are studied in the participating schools and colleges.
- raise their awareness of the opportunities that higher education will offer them.
- recognise that higher education is possible, affordable, exciting and enjoyable, through their direct contact with their mentors.
- draw up and implement individual learning plans, to include personal achievement targets and timescales for action.
- acquire and develop study skills in order to improve their application to their studies.
- develop and improve their self-esteem, motivation, confidence, persistence, application and time management.

There exist no significant technical obstacles to such a programme's adoption: there is rich evidence of similar programmes' efficacy. Nor would there be lack of support in universities. All that is missing are politicians with the imagination and active social concern to recognize the potential for transformation of individual mentors' and mentees' lives and life chances; for the measurable and non-measurable successes of the UK's education systems; and who are willing to act as policy champions and entrepreneurs. Given the punishing economic and cultural cost of concentrated educational failures within the UK, and the availability of a tested policy instrument with the demonstrated capacity to generate an attractive return upon the programme's cost, a national mentoring scheme should command the support of politicians and civil servants seeking to stretch and enthuse school students. The intensity of commitment to excellence that characterizes Britain's great universities is transferable to a mentoring scheme and is nationally scalable. Can politicians and civil servants be persuaded to sit up and take notice?

"HOME IS WHERE ONE STARTS FROM": INTOUNIVERSITY AND THE ROLE OF THE HOME ENVIRONMENT IN PUPIL ACHIEVEMENT

Rachel Carr and Hugh Rayment-Pickard

"Home is where one starts from. As we grow older
the world becomes stranger, the pattern more complicated."

T.S.Eliot, *The Four Quartets*, "Burnt Norton"

Where do the roots of the problem of educational under-achievement lie? If the prevailing wisdom is to be believed, the cause of educational failure is poor schools and poor teaching. The remedy, administered by successive governments, has been relentless school reform. In the past 20 years, since Sir Keith Joseph's Education Reform Act 1988, public policy in education has largely focussed on improving student achievement by reorganising schools, by imposing school assessment regimes and by prescribing school curricula.[1]

It is impossible to disagree with the argument that good schools and good teaching are important, but the focus of public attention and resources on schools has obscured the role that families and other agencies play in educational achievement. Policy makers have assumed too readily that school-based strategies will in the end be successful, but this assumption has not been sufficiently scrutinised and questioned.

It is true that in some respects schools policy has been effective. For example, the proportion of deprived children (those on Free School Meals) who

---

[1] For an analysis of school reforms, see Bernard Barker, "School reform policy in England since 1988: relentless pursuit of the unattainable." *Journal of Education Policy* 23: 6 (November 2008), 669–683. As he argues: "The policy mix of choice, competition, markets, regulation, accountability and leadership seems not to have closed the gap between advantaged and disadvantaged areas and individuals, while most variations in school performance can be explained in terms of intake differences."

get 5 or more good GCSEs including English and Maths has gone up from under 15% in 2002 to 23.5% in 2008. This is a worthy achievement.

But there have also been some notable failures. Peter Tymms and Christine Merrell have argued that despite a Government investment of half a billion pounds on the National Literacy Strategy between 1998 and 2005, there was "almost no impact on reading levels".[2] This must at least make policy-makers ask whether there needs to be a review of how and where public funds are invested. Tymms and Merrell conclude that:

> "we know surprisingly little about the long term and, in many cases, the short-term educational consequences of recent government initiatives and strategic changes. We are not short of opinion on 'what works', and there is a growing body of post-hoc research and evaluation, but we are short of firm evidence."

Firm evidence for school-based initiatives may be scarce but there is a considerable body of research showing schools are by no means the most important factor in a child's education. US economist and Nobel laureate James Heckman argues that:

> "schools work with what parents give them. The 1966 Coleman Report on inequality in school achievement clearly documented that the major factor explaining the variation in the academic performance of children across U.S. schools is the variation in parental environments—*not* the variation in per pupil expenditure across schools or pupil-teacher ratios. Successful schools build on the efforts of successful families. Failed schools deal in large part with children from dysfunctional families that do not provide the enriched home environments enjoyed by middle class and upper middle class children."[3]

On this side of the Atlantic a study by academics at University College London and King's College London revealed that a child's social background is

---

[2] Peter Tymms and Christine Merrell, "Standards and Quality in English Primary Schools over Time", *Primary Review* Research Report 4: 1 (2007).

[3] James J. Heckman and Dimitriy V. Masterov, "The Productivity Argument for Investing in Young Children", National Bureau for Economic Research, Working Paper No. 13016 (2007). Heckman makes the point powerfully, but the link between underachievement and home circumstances has been the subject of academic research for the past 50 years. E. Fraser (1959) and J.W.B Douglas (*The Home and the School,* 1964) and the Plowden Report (CACE 1967) found a strong correlation between attainment and parental interest in education. Plowden concluded that parental attitudes were the most significant factor in achievement.

the crucial factor in academic performance, and that a school's success is based overwhelmingly on the class background of its pupils.[4]

These findings suggest that there is a need to trial and research educational initiatives that compensate for the deficit in aspiration and enrichment within the home environment.

The climate is arguably starting to change. There is a cross-party consensus now that Third Sector agencies may have an important role not only in delivering education projects beyond the school environment, but in the innovation of new educational practice. *Overcoming the Barriers to Higher Education*, a report commissioned by HEFCE, concluded:

"Given that it is possible to predict with alarming accuracy the qualifications of individuals at age 16 and their chances of staying on in education simply from what is known about them at birth, we need to direct our resources more towards families and wider society."[5]

At **Into**University we have innovated an education project that gives poorer children some of the advantages that are enjoyed by their peers in more affluent families, helping them to hold their own in an increasingly competitive educational world.

In many middle-class homes young people can expect to receive sustained educational support including:

- Specialist tuition, particularly to help with secondary transfer and exam preparation: The private tutorial market in the UK is estimated to be worth £100 million a year.[6] According to a 2009 MORI poll, almost half of young people in London (43 per cent) reported receiving some form of private tuition.[7]
- Holidays, hobbies, trips, cultural outings and other "enrichment" activities.

---

[4] R. Webber and T. Butler, "Classifying pupils by where they live: how well does this predict variations in their GCSE results?" CASA Working Paper Number 99, University College London (2006).
[5] S Gorard et al, *Overcoming the Barriers to Higher Education,* Trentham Books (2007) p.129.
[6] J. Henry and A. Mourant, "Three-year-olds are sent to private tutors", *The Daily Telegraph* (26 Nov 2006).
[7] "A research study among 11-16 year olds on behalf of the Sutton Trust", Ipsos MORI (2009).

- Home environments rich in educational materials such as books: Research by the National Literacy Trust found that poor pupils had fewer books at home than their wealthier peers and reported that their parents read less with their children and give them less encouragement to read.[8]   An OECD survey showed that the number of books in the home correlates directly with later reading competence.[9]

- Parental and other family experience of Higher Education: children in poor homes are much less likely to have parents who have been to university. In our experience many young people from deprived homes have very low levels of awareness of what a university is or of what benefits a university education might bring.

- Parental expectations of children are significantly lower in poorer homes. Only 4% of middle class parents expect their child to "peak" at GCSE compared with 25% of poorer parents. Only 14% of poorer parents expect their children to go into Higher Education.[10]

Typically, in high aspiration homes young people will be exposed to the powerful expectations of parents and are likely to have influential role models in the wider family. Naturally, young people with these cultural and social advantages are much better placed to follow their elders into HE and the professions. Indeed, the UK school leavers who are likely to make it into the professions will come from the 30% most affluent families.[11]

The **Into**University programme works with young people and their parents and offers a mix of academic support, mentoring and special study weeks in order to compensate for the deficit of aspiration and learning support in the home environment. The service operates over the long term, providing continuing support to young people through to university access. The programme is run from specialist centres where young people can receive the year-on-year motivation, encouragement and high expectation that more affluent students are likely to enjoy as a matter of course. The centres also provide an alternative reference group of fellow students, rich in aspiration and with strongly positive attitudes to learning.

---

[8] C. Clark, C. and R. Akerman, *Social inclusion and reading: An exploration.* London: National Literacy Trust (2006).

[9] Irwin S. Kirsch, *Reading for change: performance and engagement across countries: results from PISA 2000*, OECD Publishing (2002), at 131.

[10] "Creating a high aspiration culture for young people in the UK", Ipsos MORI research for The Sutton Trust (2006).

[11] *Unleashing Aspiration*, Cabinet Office (July 2009).

Most widening participation projects start with young people over the age of 14. We believe that this is too late and that attitudes to HE have already been formed by this age. The authors of *Overcoming the Barriers to Higher Education* also reached this conclusion:

"To be fully effective, interventions need to occur early in life. Interventions in post-16 participation and in the process of application to HE face a greater challenge to make headway in changing the subjective opportunity structure of the individual."[12]

IntoUniversity starts working with young people as young as 7 in order to plant the seeds of aspiration and university awareness at an early stage. Our FOCUS programme working with primary-age students is a carefully constructed educational intervention over several years culminating (at Year 6) in a full week of activities designed to get young people thinking about the future pathways to their academic and professional success. In the course of the programme, young people will visit a university and work in teams on a university-style learning project on a focussed topic. The FOCUS programme enables young people to see their present learning in the context of a progression to higher education, and provides a framework for future aspirations. All participants enjoy a university visit to experience at first hand their potential future and young people finish the programme knowing *what* a university is, *why* they should aspire to go there and *what* they need to do academically to realise this aspiration.

Alongside this, our after school academic support programme offers young people practical support to improve their attainment and a space where they can receive pastoral as well as academic support. With one adult for every five students and the opportunity for much one-to-one support, young people receive high quality after-school help. Students agree targets and are regularly assessed to ensure that they are making good progress.

In order that our students have positive role-models, we also provide opportunities for mentoring with undergraduates and young professionals. Mentors typically meet with students every two weeks to discuss their future ambitions and to receive encouragement with their studies.

In addition, our centres work with secondary schools to provide a series of special workshops and out-of-school programmes which aim to give young people knowledge about university life and the aspiration to obtain a university place. Our experience shows that in poorer homes there is often only a very

---

[12] Gorard et al, *Overcoming the Barriers to Higher Education* Trentham Books (2007), p.122.

sketchy understanding of the benefits of a higher education and little encouragement given to children to set their sights at that level.

Taken as a whole, the **Into**University programme makes a significant impact on a young person's life, providing inspiring adult role models, setting high expectations, giving specialist knowledge and support with learning. It is precisely these factors that put middle-class children at such a huge advantage. Without the kind of support provided by **Into**University, students from poorer homes find it very hard to compete for the finite number of HE places available each year.

A recent survey of our stakeholders, including school and university partners, parents and volunteers revealed that the impact of the **Into**University education programme is not limited to our students. Families commented on the impact of the programme on home life through improved attitudes. The **Into**University partnership with one university college was noted as "crucial ... as it links with the college's wider strategic objectives". Those who volunteer on the programme reported benefits including confirmation of "my future plans of working with young people ... something I was unsure of pursuing".

Schools also benefitted. One teacher commented that "more and more students want to become involved with **Into**University and can really see the value of working hard at school and reaping the rewards at university and beyond"; another noted that:

> "Those students who have been taking part are now really good role models and are much more focused on their studies than before and really want to gain good grades as they can see the importance of higher education. IU also promotes a greater sense of citizenship and awareness of the community. We also know IU increases self confidence and self respect."

As things currently stand, vast numbers of talented young people never see their aptitudes realised simply because of their home circumstances. Potential doctors are working in supermarkets and potential barristers are working as baristas. This is tragic enough for the young people concerned, but it is also a wasteful and inefficient use of resources.

There is a pressing need for public policy makers in education to broaden their gaze beyond schools so that new kinds of work, like ours, can be researched and developed to address the educational deficit in the home environment.

SOCIAL EXCLUSION AND UNDERACHIEVEMENT: THE EASTSIDE STORY

Ray Lewis

Beginnings

8 years ago I began to lay the foundations for developing an extended schools project that blossomed into the Eastside Young Leaders' Academy (EYLA). EYLA exists to nurture and develop the potential of young African and Caribbean males. We provide educational and emotional support for boys aged 8-18, particularly those identified as being at risk of social exclusion.

The academy operates within a nexus of strong partnerships with local schools, community groups and the private sector. In the case of the last, EYLA's partnership with corporates and local businesses ensures the boys have exposure to the world of work and high profile business leaders. We focus on respect and self worth, inculcating a culture of hard work, academic excellence and civic responsibility. We seek to develop the interpersonal skills of each child, instilling in them self confidence and unlocking their creative flair.

Eastside is based in Newham, East London 5 miles east of the City of London. It is a challenging borough for a number of reasons. It has one of the highest ethnic minority populations and one of the lowest white British populations. With the highest young population it "boasts" the busiest youth court in the country.

The educational indices show similar problems. Newham has the highest proportion of population between 16 and 74 without any qualifications at all of any borough in London. 13% of the children have a special needs statement. In 2007/8 Newham's rate of permanent school exclusions was well above the national average. Few black boys stay on at secondary school.

Working exclusively with black boys in East London we are often embroiled in the nebulous debate as to "who finished last: black boys vs. white boys". In the race to the bottom this question ignores the fact that the mainstream school agenda is a massive irrelevance for many students, especially for those with serious issues in their home and communities.

Background

There is an endless stream of research on the disadvantages and social exclusion experienced by young black men in the UK. Examples of the need for effective intervention include:

- The percentage of black children achieving grades A-C at GCSE is well below the national average.
- Unemployment amongst black African and Caribbean people is 9% higher than the national average.
- In 2004 there were just 6 Black directors working for FTSE 100 companies, 3 more than in 2001.
- Black boys are six times more likely to be excluded from school than their white counterparts.
- The black population of England is 4.6%, yet the percentage of black prisoners is almost 17%. Meanwhile, black students account for just 3% of undergraduates.

Under-achievement amongst African Caribbean males has been a serious issue since the Windrush generation of the 1950s. Intervention initiatives have been in existence almost as long and significantly since the 1960s. At present there are more than 1500 so called Supplementary or Saturday schools in the UK.

Successive generations of BME communities have recognised that education is the only legitimate opportunity for social mobility amongst poorer communities.

Battles

The above notwithstanding, the barriers and battles towards a dynamic, egalitarian system of education remain problematic, resulting in increasing numbers of the socially excluded (both black and white).

Social exclusion is a process and a dynamic one. It is a systematic and structural deprivation of an individual's opportunity to participate in society. Sadly too many black boys and their families opt for active social exclusion. They lay claim to identities and lifestyles that compound their disadvantage and existence on the margins of society.

Eastside exists and works in this context.

Perhaps the great struggle is the battle of expectations or aspirations. On the subject of raising aspirations, one black Head Master said to me in 2007, "Ray, many of my students and their families have been down for so long, getting up doesn't cross their mind".

The Education Consultant, Professor Gus John, was keynote speaker at the launch of EYLA. Amongst the things he spoke of was the sad and significant culture of underachievement amongst black boys. That culture contributed to "the sort of mayhem in our communities that we have seen in recent times – with black boys being stabbed to death. There is a culture of low expectations on the part of the boys themselves and those who taught them. Many of the parents themselves have been schooled in a culture of low aspirations".

In recent years EYLA has developed a robust and fruitful partnership with Rugby School in Warwickshire. Through this connection and its bond with the Arnold Foundation, 5 of our students have gained scholarships.

One of our young leaders, Marcus, was asked to comment on some aspect of life at Rugby that struck him as significant, helpful or otherwise. He went on to say that he had been greatly affected by the aspirations of the other students from more privileged backgrounds. Specifically he said; "the boys in my school all aspire to be at least as successful as their parents; in my home there are no such aspirations. I compensate for this by competing with them to see if I have what it takes." If it is true that children seldom rise above the aspirations of their parents, then Marcus's revelation is daunting.

The above was further underlined at a meeting of Eastside parents held in 2008 to discuss their roles in support of their children's learning. Of the 25 parents in attendance there was only one that had attended university. Most of the parents had participated in short courses, in-service training and other examples but the idea or even the ideal of university for their children, was not something they had given serious consideration. Through conversation and debate I discovered that these parents, mainly black, were fearful of such places. Further education was un-charted waters; part of the culture of delayed gratification. One parent put it thus "Ray, as far as I was concerned I wanted my son to join Eastside because I didn't think he would make it through school. I didn't make it and I wanted him to make it. School is something you have to get through; doing well is an added extra. University is well...... a different world"

EYLA attempts to build bridges between these worlds, the world as it is and the world as we would like it to be. Students spend an average of 15 hours a week at the Academy. In all aspects of the programme the emphasis on early intervention, respect and self-worth are inculcating a culture of hard work, academic excellence and community involvement amongst the boys. This is supplemented by essential and appropriate parental support. We seek to build the academic and interpersonal skills of our young leaders, instilling self-confidence and unlocking creative flair. Visits to corporations and places of cultural interest build their soft skills and cultural capital.

Alongside the above EYLA recruits and trains male role models who are important in the social and emotional development of our young men. We call it positive masculinity designed and deployed to counter the negative exposure and also the absence of dads. Eastside staff and tutors are both male and female; the sex and race of teachers is not as important as their ability to teach and their credibility in relating.

Martin is a handsome and bright boy who came to EYLA when he was nine years old. He had obviously been bored at school, misapplying his energy and creating his own entertainment. He challenged everything at home and school and would never accept anything his parents or teachers told him without evidence. He wouldn't obey rules save that which he established for himself and the whole class followed his lead.

Frequently excluded from school, Martin's behaviour became steadily more difficult and dangerous. Despite his age and lack of progress in school he quickly learned the language and qualifications of the street. He was on the starting block of that downhill race into drugs, gangs and criminal behaviour. Martin was referred to us by his head teacher in September 2004 and he recalls his first day as the most daunting experience in his whole life. "I remember someone said *no* to me in a way I had never heard it before." He discovered boundaries and that things like respect were non-negotiable. Martin's transformation was dramatic and he is a leader of leaders; still handsome and bright but now focussed and diligent. His dream today, aged 15, is to win a place at Oxford University.

The pluses and prospect of going to college or university is countered by the discomfort of being in a different environment. This tension is part of the preparatory work and the heart of social mobility. Blazing a trail in this arena is the work of Patrick Derham (Head Master of Rugby) through the Arnold Foundation. My earlier mention of Marcus is an example of this revolution. His experiences as a Scholarship Student defy convention by merging cultures into a melting pot of aspiration, inspiration and mutuality.

Belief

The culture and philosophy underpinning the work of Eastside is the belief that the value of each child is based on their potential rather than their need.

Further educational deprivation is socially corrosive but professional educators can make a difference.

Families that join EYLA are looking for a sense of community; a place to belong, somewhere that replaces the home that many have lost. They join because they are tired of suffering in isolation. What they find is a place that is organised and honest; where words like "integrity", "intention" and "commitment" are not merely nouns, but verbs.

We appreciate the fact that parents are responsible for the hopes and aspirations of their children but it's a short step from fostering the mentality of blame. Our experience is that when parents are fully engaged, challenged and encouraged, lives are transformed.

I have no wish to exaggerate the importance of what we do, nor indeed to take our experiences and make it a principle. We all feel very privileged to be involved in this work and have seen marvellous things. We have our detractors and dissenters alongside families and individuals whose experience of EYLA has not been the most edifying.

London is a city comprising of many self-appointed gurus and mystics representing a myriad of competing ideologies especially in the field of education where all too often our children are caught in the middle.

Social exclusion results in the abandonment of hope and the death of aspiration, this in turn is not easily overcome. Eastside works hard to counter this. In all our endeavours EYLA is careful not to create dependency or propagate the message that the value of our young people lies in their deficiencies. EYLA is not an organisation built upon people's needs. EYLA is about community not service, capacity not deficiency. These beliefs drive our programmes.

UNLEASHING ASPIRATION

Patrick Derham

Unleashing aspiration should be the raison d'être of all educational institutions. *Unleashing Aspirations*[1] is also the striking title of Alan Milburn's report and although there is much in the report to applaud, its criticisms that the independent sector acts as a brake on social mobility are misguided, as Rudolf Eliott Lockhart argued in a recent ISC Bulletin.[2] Many independent schools were founded with charitable intent and have, throughout their history, provided transformational opportunities for their pupils, advancing the cause of social mobility. Lots of schools provide bursaries but I believe Rugby School's approach is radically different. In this chapter I want to consider why, what we are doing at Rugby, has attracted a great deal of interest from politicians, the media, parliamentary committees and, perhaps most importantly, from other independent schools who have been keen to learn from our experiences.

Context is important. Social mobility is not an abstract concept for me. My father was a soldier and after he left the Army my family moved to a council estate in the Borders of Scotland. When I was 12 I was a pupil onboard the Training Ship Arethusa which was run by The Shaftesbury Homes and I was destined to leave full-time education for a career in the Navy at the age of 16. My life was turned upside down when through charitable support I found myself at Pangbourne College, a school that offered me a whole new world of opportunities and instead of leaving school at 16 I went on to read history at Cambridge. I can say with confidence that without this opportunity I would not be sitting at the desk of my celebrated predecessor, Dr Arnold, who himself was a passionate believer in the redemptive power of education.

My experience means that I not only recognise the truth of the great Chartist slogan that "education is a liberating force" but I am also passionately committed

---

[1] Unleashing Aspiration: The Final report of the Panel on Fair Access to the Professions (London, 2009).
[2] ISC Bulletin 25 (London November 2009).

to broadening access. I believe that schools have a duty to give as many young people as possible similar life-changing opportunities. Widening access is very much part of Rugby's DNA and since the school was founded in 1567, Rugby has provided support for day pupils through the Lawrence Sheriff bequest. When I came to Rugby in 2001 I wanted to provide the same opportunities for boarding pupils and so in 2003 the Arnold Foundation was established to offer fully funded places, subject to means testing, to young people who would particularly benefit from a boarding school education but who are unable to afford the fees. Where necessary Arnold Foundation support includes the cost of extras, for example uniform, laptop, essential books, trips and travel to and from the school. All our fund-raising is directed at providing transformational opportunities for young people. We have come a long way in 6 years. To date more than £6.6 million has been raised and there are currently 24 pupils in the school supported by the Arnold Foundation. Since the scheme started 42 pupils have benefitted from the Foundation's support with 12 already pursuing a university education. So, what can we learn from The Arnold Foundation?

The most important lesson is that to be really effective, bursary programmes must stem from a genuine desire to transform lives. The Arnold Foundation was not a knee-jerk response to the Charities Act (2006) but is part of a genuine commitment to widening access at Rugby. This tradition was started by the founder, Lawrence Sheriff, pursued by Heads such as Arnold and Percival, and continues to the present day. Independent research has found that Rugby's long tradition of charitable activity is a key factor in the scheme's success. The Arnold Foundation is "embedded in an egalitarian and inclusive school culture."[3] Not only do Arnold Foundation pupils benefit from this culture (it helps them settle in and feel part of the school) but the Arnold Foundation in turn reinforces Rugby's founding values and ethos. Rugby's other pupils benefit from the social diversity and insight into less privileged backgrounds, and the staff find working with Arnold Foundation pupils particularly rewarding.[4]

The Arnold Foundation needs to be seen in the context of changing attitudes to scholarships and bursaries. Scholarships should be directed to those who need them and not given to the bright or talented children of the wealthy. I was determined that we should lead in this important respect and Rugby was the first boarding school to reduce all our scholarships to 10% in 2003 but at the same time to make all scholarships fully augmentable to 100% support subject to means-testing. John Clare commented in *The Daily Telegraph* that "other schools have no excuse not to follow suit", and Dick Davison, writing in *The Independent*, described

---

[3] National Foundation for Educational Research Evaluation of the Arnold Foundation for Rugby School (January 2010), page 42.
[4] op.cit., page 24.

what we were doing as "a striking response".[5]   Rugby's belief that independent schools can and should be powerful engines of social mobility is demonstrated by a clearly stated aim of having 10% of pupils funded either through the Lawrence Sheriff bequest, for day pupils, or through the Arnold Foundation for those in boarding places within the next 10 years.

The second key lesson we have learnt is the importance of finding the right pupils to support. We are not interested in using bursaries simply to cherry pick the brightest children from maintained schools. Instead we want to help those who stand to gain the most from a boarding education and who can later become role models and leaders within their own communities. We do not advertise for pupils but work principally with partner organisations; we know this is crucial to our success. We are innovative in that we have sought out educational charities in inner-city areas who are dealing first-hand with the very real issues of social exclusion and underachievement and who share our commitment to raise aspirations.

Our two most established alliances are with **Into**University[6] and the Eastside Young Leaders' Academy. The former is a pioneering educational charity which uses a range of out-of-school programmes and works with children as young as 7 in its centres in deprived areas of London to achieve its core purpose to raise aspirations to help more young people from poor homes to go to university. Eastside Young Leaders' Academy aims to nurture leadership potential in an effort to improve the life chances of young African and Caribbean boys and like **Into**University starts with primary school children. Working with these charities has been central to our success as it enables us to reach out to young people for whom boarding is a remote concept. These organisations help in identifying suitable candidates and are fully involved in the whole application process. The majority of Arnold Foundation pupils are from a single parent family, and may have to contribute to running the household, or live in cramped and noisy accommodation where it is difficult to study. Boarding at Rugby liberates them from these constraints and provides them with the support and encouragement they need to achieve their full potential. There are plans to strengthen and to widen the partnerships that support the Arnold Foundation to create opportunities for even more children from diverse backgrounds. Already we have a pupil from Future Hope[7] in Kolkata which in its work with street children who have little or no ability to change their lives provides a home, education medical aid and most

---

[5] *The Daily Telegraph* (24th March 2004); *Independent* (13th October 2005)

[6] The outstanding work of **Into**University and of the Eastside Young Leaders' Academy is covered in detail in this book in the essays by Carr and Rayment-Pickard and by Lewis respectively. .

[7] Information on Future Hope can be found on www.futurehope.net.

importantly opportunity. Links are being developed in Hong Kong and America as well as in other parts of the UK.

What our partner organisations believe in, as do we at Rugby, is that it is a long-term pastoral engagement with young people that is crucial to improving performance and therefore in raising aspirations. This then is the third key lesson we have learnt. Pastoral support is critical to a bursary scheme's success and this support must be for families as well as for the young people. For the pupils they not only receive school-based support but also on-going support from the partner charities. At school they have the same pastoral support as all pupils but in addition to this they benefit from having older peers as mentors and they also have access to three dedicated Arnold Foundation tutors. Key to the success of this is the understanding and empathy the tutors have with the Arnold Foundation pupils, and their awareness of the pupils' home environment.[8] The Deputy Head at Rugby works closely with the three tutors and also oversees the progress of the Arnold Foundation pupils. It is interesting that the pupils are so well integrated that many Rugbeians and staff don't know which pupils at Rugby are supported by the Arnold Foundation. We want the parents to also share in the journey and so we have a parent coordinator who sees the Arnold Foundation parents on a regular basis and who is always happy to talk to the families. She is able to offer independent support and advice. The partner organisations help in this respect too and so parents, like the pupils, are encouraged to embrace all that Rugby has to offer. Most importantly this level of support is maintained during the school holidays and the transition between school and home is carefully managed.

Transforming lives is at the heart of the Arnold Foundation and our aspiration has become a reality. Arnold Foundation pupils have achieved academic success and of the pupils who have left Rugby one is a professional rugby player and all the others are either at University (including one Arnold Foundation pupil who came to us through **Into**University and who is now reading History at Pembroke College Cambridge) or on a GAP Year. NFER research has found the benefits of attending Rugby for Arnold Foundation pupils includes increased academic achievement and extracurricular participation, improved social skills and self-esteem, development of leadership skills, enhanced social skills, aspiration to go on to Higher Education and increased confidence.[9] For some, the Arnold Foundation has been an opportunity to break free from negative cycles such as gang culture, financial pressure, and a culture of low educational attainment and low aspirations.[10] Furthermore the NFER research found the Arnold Foundation

---

[8] National Foundation for Educational Research Evaluation of the Arnold Foundation for Rugby School (January 2010), page 48.

[9] op. cit., page 5.

[10] op. cit., page 20.

impacts on pupils' "perceptions of what is possible to achieve in their lives. Pupils feel their horizons have been broadened and that they can do whatever they want if they work hard enough for it." As one Arnold Foundation pupil said "I don't know what I want to be yet – but I know I could do what I want to do. The world is my oyster really."

The Arnold Foundation is unique because it is so carefully targeted. By offering places to young people who stand to gain the most and who have the potential to become role models in their own communities, Rugby is helping to raise aspirations at a much broader level. The NFER research found that the partner organisations we work with use the achievements of their Arnold Foundation pupils to raise the aspirations of the other young people they work with. The significance of what we are doing was brought home to us when David Davies, the then Shadow Home Secretary, mentioned Rugby and our work with the Eastside Young Leaders' Academy, as a positive example of what can be done through bursary support when he spoke at the Conservative Party Conference in 2007. In fact David Davies said something that I think is at the heart of what the Arnold Foundation is about when he ended by saying that what we are doing demonstrates "that no matter where you come from, there's no limit to how high you can climb."[11] One pupil who came originally from a maintained school in Newport said "they have pictures of me up on the wall at school in my [Rugby] school uniform. It just shows that this place opens doors."[12] The Head of a maintained school in Scotland said that no independent school in Scotland had ever spoken to him professionally but he wanted to be associated with Rugby because of our shared values and aspirations and that the link with Rugby was an opportunity for his pupils that could only bring benefits to all concerned. The same sentiments have also been expressed by Heads of maintained schools in London. Families too report their pride in their children's achievements and in some cases, the aspirations of other family members and even the local community has been raised.[13]

We know that what we are doing is transforming lives and unleashing aspiration. I want to finish with a speech given at our 5th Anniversary celebration in May 2008 by an Arnold Foundation pupil who took her A Levels shortly afterwards. What she said on that occasion sums up perfectly for me that what we are providing is really making a difference:

"I'm 18 years old and I am an Arnold Foundationer at Rugby School. For the past 12 years I have studied and lived in London. My previous school was in the bottom 5% of all London schools. This small statistic may give

---

[11] 2007 Conservative Party Conference Speech (Blackpool).
[12] op. cit., page 28.
[13] op. cit., page 29.

you an idea about the academic differences I experienced upon coming to Rugby. After living in London for 15 years I decided to leave home, I wanted to drop out of school, I didn't want A-levels and I had no inclination to ever go to university. After continuous problems at home I went in to foster care, I was 15 at the time and it was here that I was informed about the Arnold Foundation. I was urged to apply as many people close to me did not want to see me throw my life away. I was wary at first about applying as I felt there was no chance of me getting accepted, however I did want things to change in my life and felt that Rugby would be the best place to have a fresh start. I really had no idea how much Rugby would alter my life; I have met people I would never have spoken to and made friends I wouldn't trade in for anything. I have always been interested in Drama but have never really had the facilities around me to really experiment with different styles and techniques, the Macready theatre has been a great asset to my study of acting and the theatre. Similarly the ability to do photography A-level had never been offered to me before and since taking it have found something I am quite passionate about. Something else the Arnold Foundation has given me is the ability to travel. Just recently I travelled to America with the school on a politics trip. Over a week we stayed in Washington DC and New York, meeting a number of Congressmen and sitting in on a Senate meeting. Rugby has also made me want to go on to further education and after being accepted in to all 5 of my University choices I have decided to go to Edinburgh University. The Arnold Foundation has shown me that with determination, no matter what background you're from, anyone can succeed and get the most out of an education that everyone deserves."

The Arnold Foundation is a bursary scheme that is achieving so much more than simply helping out with school fees.